Remember the Dragonflies

A Memoir of Grief and Healing

To Bob and Yvonne —

Kathy Rhodes

Kathy Rhodes

WestBow
PRESS
A DIVISION OF THOMAS NELSON

WestBow Press books may be ordered through booksellers or by contacting:

WestBow Press
A Division of Thomas Nelson
1663 Liberty Drive
Bloomington, IN 47403
www.westbowpress.com
1 (866) 928-1240

ISBN: 978-1-4908-1076-8 (sc)
ISBN: 978-1-4908-1077-5 (hc)
ISBN: 978-1-4908-1075-1 (e)

Printed in the United States of America.

WestBow Press rev. date: 09/30/2013

For my family: Corey, Ellison, Jillie, Hardy, Judi, and David

And in loving memory of my parents, Ray and
Lucille Hardy, and, of course, my husband, Charlie
Rhodes, who walked home to God with me

"My hope is that each of us—in our own way and in our own time—will find a resting place far away from this sorrow."

T. E. Belt

Contents

A Note About This Book

This is a work of nonfiction. It is an honest account of my feelings, emotions, and experiences during and after the death of my loved one. As a creative nonfiction writer—a writer of true stories—I did not make anything up or embellish in any way. I tried to fact-check my memory because I was pulling things up from five years ago or more. I tried my best to be accurate with scenes, characters, and dialogue.

I re-remembered and re-played each scene in my mind. Nothing was fabricated. The characters are all real people in real situations. No characters were invented. Mostly, real names were used; however, in a few instances, names or spellings were changed, but the person represented by the name was true to life. I tried to be true to dialogue; if not the exact words, then the gist was presented in a manner that was true to the character.

I relied on entries from the blog I have maintained since October, 2007. These entries provide real, raw, in-the-moment feelings of grief, as well as accurate details.

This is a story about my life, and this is the way I remember it.

Acknowledgments

My deepest thanks to my sister, Judi Hardy Shellabarger, who told me the night my husband died that I had to build a whole new life. Then she traveled with me every summer after that and helped me do it.

My sincere thanks also to my brother-in-law, David Rhodes, who calls me every couple of weeks, comes to check on me every couple of months, and told me I needed to have faith in God.

Thanks also to Judy Hurley for her unwavering encouragement and support as we worked through our grief journeys together, her husband Jim having died five months before my Charlie.

A big thanks to my writers group for always being there with encouragement, support, and criticism: Susie Dunham, Chance Chambers, Jack Wallace, and Neil O. Jones. And thanks to Neil for helping me between critique sessions by offering his superb professorial advice, helping me move to my brand new house, and helping me to have fun again.

Thanks to my sons Ellison and Corey for being there for me and for being such awesome men. Thanks to Ellison for calling to check on me every day for a year and to Corey who called every day for five years and beyond. Thanks to my dog Chaeli for being such a warm, wonderful companion.

And thank you to all the grief support groups I attended and drew strength and lifeblood from: the GriefShare groups at Christ Presbyterian Church, Nashville, Tennessee, and Brentwood Baptist Church, Brentwood, Tennessee, and to Alive Hospice at First United Methodist Church, Brentwood.

I also express my gratitude to Stephanie Mendel for letting me quote from her book of poems, *March, before Spring*, which captures the devastation of losing a spouse and offers comfort and hope to those who have gone through intense grief after such a loss.

A chapter from this book, "An Open Letter," first appeared in *The Best Creative Nonfiction, Volume 3*, edited by Lee Gutkind, published by W. W. Norton & Company, 2009.

Existential

Charlie Rhodes, 1994

Open your eyes and dream . . .
    All the dreams you've not yet dared.
        Of untamed passion, infinite bliss,
        Castles amid clouds of fantasy,
        Soaring with songbirds
        Over endless fields of flowers,
        Of peace, truth, love enduring.
    Realities merge, galaxies collide, existence emerging.
Life is so short. Dream often . . .
    Open your eyes and love . . .
        The pure, unbounded love of your dreams.
        Open your heart to possibilities
        Of tender caring, soul laid bare,
        Trusting, vulnerable, invincible.
        Giving, sharing, yielding—all that you have,
        All that you are, all you can and will become.
    Hearts entwine, reason abandoned, existence defined.
    Time is fleeting. Love completely . . .
Open your eyes and live . . .
    The unbridled dreams and love of your heart.
        Feel the softness, taste the sweetness
        Of all that grows in your field of dreams.
        Sing your songs of insatiable love.
        Explore the bounds of knowing.
        Exceed yourself.
Potential unfolding, forces unleashed, existence assured.
Life begins. Live it all, live it well.

Introduction

What if everything you had in your life depended on one person, and then, in the twinkling of an eye, that person was gone?

At some point life is going to boil what's in your crucible down to the salt of you.

It did to me. The unthinkable happened. Charlie died.

Charlie was the source of all the physical things I counted on: my job—I worked for him—all sources of income, identity, companionship, love, future hopes and dreams, even the house I lived in.

Grief jerked me up out of a normal life—one with plans, hugs, coffee and shared conversation every morning, laughter, and dinner with a glass of wine every evening across the table from someone I cared about—and threw me down on a different path, forcing me to go that way to some destination unmarked and unknown. Grief is disruptive. It is messy, chaotic, and mean.

Grief has been my road to walk. There are no rules to grief. We all grieve in our own way. We walk our own personal journey. The road stretches out far ahead of us, climbs the hills, drops to the valleys, covers the flatlands, scales the mountain peaks, takes curves and switchbacks and loops, cuts through canyons, and goes all the way to the ocean.

The appearance of that road reminds me of the dirt road on my grandfather's farm in Mississippi that was an old Choctaw Indian path before my great-great-grandfather settled there in 1850. When Papaw's father and uncles inherited the farm and divided it up, they used the old road to travel between the houses they built and the ponds they dug to fish in. Family wagons with heavy wheels, wooden slides pulled by mules, and footsteps that pounded the dirt for four generations wore the road down—down below the surface of the ground—and by the time I was born, it had cliff-like sides a foot high.

The grief road goes through such a worn-down place—"the valley of the shadow of death" (Psalm 23:4 King James Version)—only instead of a valley, it feels more like a trench cut deep into the earth, deeper than Papaw's road, a trench that you stand in, and the top edges are higher than your head, and the dirt walls touch your shoulders as you position sideways, and they threaten to tighten on you like a vise.

I know this deep-cut road. In a three-year period, I lost my father, mother, and husband. My husband was the one I was with every day and night, and the loss of my husband meant the loss of life as I knew it.

This book is about losing my husband.

Over the last five years since Charlie died, so many women have told me, "I couldn't make it if my husband died." They'd wince, squint, and shake their heads hard, convinced. "I lost a parent and got through that, but I couldn't go through losing a husband. I don't know what I would do." I'd always felt that way, too. Then I was slammed down on that deep-cut road and had no choice but to "make it."

This book is not a spiritual guide, though I am a spiritual person. I'm a Christian. I was born into a family of believers. I descend from long lines, maternal and paternal, of church-starters and deacons. I lived the clichés: cut my teeth on a pew, went to church every time the doors were open, walked the aisle to accept Jesus. Before death came, and in fact, through most of my youth and adulthood, my life was wrapped up in a tidy box with a pretty bow around it. Things went smoothly, I felt that God protected me, and there was an easy answer for everything, a clear reason attached to whatever happened. But when that death package arrived, the paper around it was all crumpled and torn and dirty, and there was no ribbon. It didn't look like something God would give me. I knew I needed to tear off that wrapping paper, open the box, and take hold of what was inside. The whole of my being was in that box—a composite of knowledge, wisdom, all my life experiences with God and people, faith, answered and unanswered prayers, all I was and had grown to be—and this was what I would hold fast to as I journeyed through grief and what ultimately would help me make it.

In order to heal, I instinctively knew I had to let myself feel my grief. I didn't want anything to mask or cover up my pain. I had to bear it alone. Nobody, no family member, no friend, not anyone could make the hurting stop. I knew God always promised a light for the way, but I believed God expected me to put forth the effort to walk that road and heal. And Psalm 23:4 affirmed it: "Yea, though I WALK . . . ."

Because I am a person of faith, I knew God was with me, in me, part of my foundation, my fabric, my core. But I had to meet my grief headfirst, shoulder into it, and push myself down that road.

Grief is a journey. And there is no travel guide.

This book is my journey—a real and honest account of what I went through and how I felt at points along the way, a spiritual struggle as I stood alone at first and then softened to the light, and a very personal pilgrimage as I discovered exactly who I am now and what I'm made of. This book is also for all the women who say, "I couldn't make it if I lost my husband." It is my hope that my journey will help you gain insight and find your way when it is your turn, or that it will speak to you if you are on that road right now or have walked that road before me.

Your journey will be different. You will navigate your own road, as I have navigated mine. You will face different barriers, bridges, mountain curves with no guardrails, ravines off to the side. If you are a person of faith, you may feel closer to God, or you may feel cut off from God. You may question God. You may question yourself. Learning to examine your feelings and your faith, learning to grapple with grief, is learning to live again. There will be a paradigm shift. There will be a new normal. You will build a whole new life.

You can do this.

With all that you are and all that you have within you, you can endure.

You can make it, too.

I Built

T he back yard was stone-solid sienna clay when I bought this new house in December, seven months ago. Fescue seeds had been scattered on top of it and covered with straw. Spring rains wet the clay and pounded the straw into it to mesh as part of the earth's hardscape, and the summer sun baked it. Pottery, that's what it was.

The landscape of my heart was pottery, too. I couldn't dig or pry the straw out of that hard clay, nor could I remove the scars left by the death of my husband.

Today—four years, one month, and one day after Charlie died—I worked nine hours in the back yard with just short breaks from the hundred-degree sun. I stood on the deck's long boards, already cupping from the heat, and looked out over the yard, a wide but shallow rectangle with a scalloped cedar fence around it. Before I moved in, it was a wild field with deer and turkeys. Feral cats roamed over it, and a neighbor told me a skunk had lived under a pile of scrap wood on my lot. Then a bulldozer's blade scraped away the untamed growth and exposed the rancid clay-dirt. I had to buy rubber muck boots before I could even work in this slippery quicksand-when-wet, pottery-when-dry mess.

Once the two maples, crape myrtle, hemlock, and tulip poplar reached full stature, they'd fill up the yard. The landscaping—seven trees, twenty-eight bushes, and about that many kinds of perennial flowers—I put in by myself, except for help with three big trees. I

1

had to dig in that awful, rubbery clay-dirt. Rainwater wouldn't soak in, but just sit inch-deep on top of it, and what little finally did settle in stayed there beneath the surface, so the roots of my plants sat in stale water. "It's like this," one of the plant experts at Riverbend Nursery told me. "When you dig a hole for a tree, you create a bowl, like a hard clay pot. When it rains, water sits in the bottom of that bowl, like milk after you eat your cereal. You've got to amend the soil to give it a healthier texture. Mix in conditioner, new dirt, and some native soil. Tamp it in tightly around the tree roots—make it solid—to keep it from having the bowl effect."

The tree needed effort, intervention, and attentive care, yet it still had to struggle to take root, stay green, and grow.

I had just finished creating a stone pathway that ran from my deck to the little vegetable garden at the back fence, where I could eat warm-off-the-vine tomatoes and peppers.

I worked too hard in the sun, hurt from carrying rocks, bending, squatting, digging, pulling weeds, and could barely lift a foot to walk up the four steps to the deck. I leaned on the railing and surveyed my handiwork. Grass was starting to sprout up out of new seeds. I wasn't sure I'd ever grow a full lawn in this unhealthy yard.

A dragonfly zoomed by close to my head. I looked up, and there were lots of them, all abuzz. They seemed desperate—in search of something. They sparkled in the sun.

I looked back to my yard. First, off the deck, heading west, there was a brick-lined, mulched walkway with six round stepping stones in it. Three had belonged to my mother before she died. My walkway went to a concrete-stone pad with a fire pit, passing a half-circle flower bed with a cobalt-blue bottle tree, a birdhouse from the Franklin Main Street Festival, and a cobalt-blue sea ball from my trip to the Oregon coast last summer, where I waded in the crashing waves of ocean water that changed to a soft, peaceful inflow.

A dragonfly dipped in front of me. Dragonflies are found in wetlands. The female lays eggs in water on floating or emergent plants. The eggs hatch, the nymphs live beneath the surface of the water, and when they are ready to change into adults, they climb up the plant, begin breathing, come out of their larval skin, and fly into the heavens.

Dragonflies have iridescent wings and bodies. They appear in different colors depending on the angle of light falling on them. This property is associated with self-discovery.

For me, the last four years have been a time of self-discovery.

When your spouse dies, your life stops. Death puts a period at the end of that last sentence of the chapter about you and your loved one. You don't know it at first, but everything that was is no more. You scramble blindly in a flood of adrenaline to pull the fractured pieces of that life in close around you within your new reality—only you do not fathom that's what you're doing.

Some people say dragonflies are the souls of the dead. Some say the deceased send us dragonflies to give us reassurance.

Beyond my fire pit was a circular herb garden fifteen feet in diameter, outlined with little paver-stones, with a square-stone pathway inside it running one side to the other and top to bottom, forming a cross, the far western point against the fence. It was plentiful with parsley, sage, rosemary, sweet mint, thyme, basil, and chives. There was a blackberry bush on a trellis against the fence.

The herb garden was designed like a medicine wheel, an ancient Native American stone formation, laid out in a circular pattern that looked like a wagon wheel, its arrangement of rocks and cairns pointing to the rising and setting places of the sun at summer solstice. Early on, Native Americans observed that there were no straight lines in nature. Nature expressed herself in circular patterns, from a bird's nest to the cycle of seasons to the cycle of life—birth, death, rebirth. Thus the wheel represented the whole universe and also one's own personal universe. It was a mirror that let one see what was going on within, how to realize and reach her potential, and how to heal. The word "medicine" referred to the power inherent in nature and to the personal power within that enabled her to become whole or complete. A medicine wheel was considered a sacred space, a place for meditation, a centering device.

A few weeks ago on summer solstice, I tried to hike with my sister to the Big Horn Medicine Wheel in Wyoming, but the trail across the steep forty-five-degree mountain slope was covered feet-deep in snow and treacherous. We couldn't make it, so we turned back. We watched the low, gray clouds of a mountain storm rush toward us, and then we laughed and danced circles in a summer snowfall.

Inside the wheel in my yard, I placed decorative personal items among the plants: a piece of the original tombstone of my Revolutionary fourth-great-grandfather John Mahaffey; a flat rock from Three Mile Creek in Ohio on land that once belonged to another Revolutionary ancestor, Jacob Boone, cousin of Daniel; and a block of wood from a pecan tree my father planted in our back yard on Deering Street when I was seven, felled by the Great Ice Storm of '94. There were two statues of little girls I took from my mother's garden and a bird bath that belonged to her. There was a painted wooden gull I bought on the Oregon coast last year, two tall handcrafted birdhouses that had doors with real, old, glass doorknobs like my Mamaw Hardy's house had, and an old rusty cow bell that came from the Hardy farm. By the thyme sat a pottery dish filled with my husband's boyhood arrowhead collection. These things represented the substance I was made of. I liked having them in my personal wheel because they reminded me who I am and where I came from.

Turning north, the stone pathway passed a bed of plants I mostly begged off my sister and friends—Siberian irises, black and blue salvia, forsythias, coreopsis, cannas, creeping jenny, and Carolina jasmine. North on the medicine wheel represented coming to my time of winter. North was wisdom, healing, a time to be grounded within myself, a time to rest and contemplate.

I built all of this. I planted every bush and flower in this yard in a desperate attempt to give life, to have life around me, to give something a chance to grow and bloom. I amended that annoying clay-soil, added nutrients, and watered to make it all healthy and make it last, because life is fragile, life is fleeting, and everyone needs a chance at life.

I sat down in the Adirondack chair and looked at the bright yellow sky with gray clouds gathered at the horizon to crown the setting sun. Dragonflies still zoomed above. They moved fast. Their life span was short. They spent most of their lives in the larva stage, and when they flew, it meant they were near the end. Right now, they were getting in all the life they could before they died. They were magical, and I wanted to reach up and touch them.

Tears rolled down my stinging-hot cheeks. I created this lush yard for the dragonflies to soar above. I wheelbarrowed in a hundred bags of topsoil and mulch, then spread it all with my bare hands. I hauled in all of these stones, four hundred three of them, and set them in place. Some of the rocks and stones I brought from my old house, the one Charlie and I built in 1994. Some came from my grandparents' farm, and I brought twelve back to Tennessee from vacation in New Mexico. The neighborhood grew still and quiet. It came to me that this was my home now.

I cried harder. Out of pain, out of pride.

My fingers were tight in the joints. Brown was worn in around the nails, dirt under them. The nails were jagged and broken. A mulch splinter was stuck down in the quick under the nail of the ring finger, left hand, the one where my wedding ring used to be.

I leaned my head against the back of the wooden chair. My hair at the roots was soaked with sweat. Traffic hummed on the interstate a half mile beyond the woods and creek in the distance. I thought about how I needed to stain and seal the deck. Needed to paint the Adirondack chairs a sea green as a contrast color to the cobalt.

Dragonflies kept buzzing and darting.

They could go forty-five miles an hour and fly in six directions. They could hover like a helicopter, fly backward like a hummingbird, fly to either side, fly straight up and down.

When your spouse dies, you are blown in all directions and you crash to the ground.

The dragonfly symbolizes maturity, change, and new beginnings.

I looked at my circular garden. The plants were tiny. I looked forward to when they mature. The rule for perennials: the first year they sleep, the second year they creep, the third year they leap.

I Didn't Know How Bad It Was

June 27, 2008

I headed for my first cup of coffee at five this Friday morning. I passed the hallway coat tree, which was packed full of winter jackets and windbreakers and even the dog's yellow raincoat, and bumped into Charlie as he was coming out the kitchen door. The nudge sent him over into the bank of coats, and he struggled to balance his coffee cup. I should have already stored that winter wear in a closet since it was officially summer. I needed to tend to lots of things, but I was busy writing and working.

"I've been up since three," he said. He was wearing his favorite worn-in pink shorts—really, burgundy-faded-to-pale-raspberry—and an orange tee shirt. He looked like a bowl of two-flavored sherbet. "I'm sick."

I put my hands on his arms and slid them into a hug. "What's wrong?" He had a deep dimple in his chin, and I couldn't resist putting the tip of my finger in there when I got close.

"My stomach."

"Stomach virus?"

"Could be."

"Do you think it could be salmonella?"

"I don't know."

We'd eaten a country summer supper a couple days earlier—peas, cornbread, chow-chow, squash, and fried okra. We'd gotten

7

fresh tomatoes from Betty Reed's open vegetable market in downtown Franklin by the Harpeth River. For the past two months, there had been a salmonella outbreak linked to tomatoes, red plum or Roma. Grocery stores had pulled them from the shelves, and restaurants had stopped serving them. Eight hundred ten people were infected in thirty-six states, six in Tennessee. Initial symptoms were abdominal cramps and diarrhea. He had both. It was a long shot, and a scary one, that he could have salmonella. People were dying from that.

Charlie was all the time picking up germs from his customers. His job was to fix their business computers and networks, do upgrades, new installations, and ironically, to clear up bugs, viruses, and other malware. He worked on the PCs of people who got sick and coughed into their hands or wiped their noses, then touched their keyboards and mice, and it's a wonder he didn't keep an infection going full time.

"Maybe it's just a twenty-four-hour thing," I said.

Downplay it. That's what I did when I didn't want to worry, when I didn't want him to worry. When I was set to fast-forward in life and I didn't take time to stop and put together the puzzle pieces scattered on the floor around me.

For months I'd had a gnawing feeling that something bad was going to happen and interrupt the life we shared: working together at GENISYS Systems Group, playing with our cocker spaniel, University of Tennessee football, fall trips to Gatlinburg, blogging, writing memoir essays, and him grilling shrimp or steaks from Butcher Block or ribs boiled in pickling spices and slathered with barbecue sauce. Every morning when I laid eyes on him—saw him pour coffee and drip nine squirts of sweetener in it, walk from the coffee pot to his desk scuffing his Lands End slippers across the hardwood, and look at the computer screen through his ten-dollar Walgreens glasses—I thanked God for at least one more day with my husband.

All the signs were there of a catastrophic event, but I was not seeing the whole picture. His color had changed. From rosacea red to chalky gray. His legs tingled. They'd never done that. His mid-back between the shoulder blades had started hurting a few days earlier.

He held his porcelain-white cowboy mug with a gray bucking bronco on it. The coffee pot was still full, so he hadn't consumed as much as he would have on a normal day. He had torn off the previous day's little square page on the Word Origin calendar I'd gotten him as a stocking stuffer for Christmas. June 27 looked back at me from the bar behind the coffee maker. One of the tall sword-shaped leaves of the snake plant next to it fell in an arch over it. I needed to water that thing so the spikes would stand up straight.

I had a schedule to keep today—a mental to-do list for GENISYS, the business Charlie had operated since 1989, when he moved to Nashville from Pittsburgh after a career with Alcoa. I'd worked with him for twelve years. This morning I had banking to do and financial reports to create. I was planning to go to Asheville Sunday because my son who'd just turned thirty was having an endoscopy on Monday. When he swallowed, he felt a lump in his throat. He'd convinced himself he had esophageal cancer. He was a worrywart anyway, but this wasn't too far-fetched. I was worried, too. He'd had acid reflux all his life, and in first grade he had an endoscopy. The gastroenterologist had said if he hadn't known the patient was six years old, he would have diagnosed Barrett's esophagus, a condition that increases the risk for developing esophageal adenocarcinoma. I needed to be with Cory through his procedure and diagnosis. If I got a stomach virus from Charlie, I couldn't go.

I poured coffee and went upstairs to my office. Writing came first in the early morning hours when my mind was fresh. Charlie went to the bedroom to his computer. He'd been blogging for four years under a penname: Winston Rand. Winston, because that's what he'd always smoked. Rand, because he liked Ayn. He sat at his oak mission desk early every morning under a framed and matted water color of the Nashville skyline that showed the Cumberland River reflecting the colors of downtown skyscrapers, including the

"Batman" Building with its tall spires and the L&C Towers where he had customers. He wrote blog posts and stories, some about his growing-up days in the West Tennessee town of Huntingdon. He wasn't supposed to be a writer. He was an electrical engineer with an MBA. He was left-brained and logical, and it wasn't fair that he could be right-brained and creative, too.

About eight, he moved to his chair in the family room, propped his feet up on the ottoman, and said, "I need you to call and cancel my customers this morning. I have two scheduled."

"You don't think you can go? You don't want to wait a while and see if you feel better?" I was the bookkeeper. He needed to go. We needed the money. I'd already told him cash flow was low, he needed to make calls on his contract clients, and he needed to make sure he'd invoiced every customer he'd been to, because income for the month of June—and June was almost over—wasn't even enough to pay my salary, much less his draw, or the office rent or other expenses. That had never happened before. The work was there. It just wasn't getting done. In the months to follow, I'd look back and wonder if his mind was slipping. He wasn't working like he usually did, and he gave me many blank looks.

"No. I told you I'm sick."

"Do we need to call the doctor?"

"Just let me sit here a while."

I called our customers to reschedule. The contact person at the business on Crossroads Boulevard expressed concern. "He's fine," I told her. "He'll be there Monday."

I prepared a deposit, then drove over Berry's Chapel Road and Lynnwood Way's high hill to the bank branch on Moore's Lane, on the other side of town. Then I drove back to the Fieldstone Farms Publix near our house and bought some ginger ale and crackers to ease Charlie's stomach. I was gone an hour.

He didn't want the ginger ale and crackers.

"I'm bleeding. There's blood with the diarrhea. And lots of it."

"I'm calling the doctor."

I sat on the old blue-and-white-flowered Clayton Marcus couch in the living room and punched in the number. We hadn't bought furniture the whole time we were married because we couldn't agree on the style. He liked contemporary. I liked traditional. So we compromised and did nothing. I got the clinic's answering machine.

"They're closed," I told Charlie. "Out to lunch. Do you think we need to call 9-1-1? That's what the message on the answering machine says to do if this is a life-threatening emergency."

"No. They'll be back by the time I shower and get my clothes on."

"Okay, we'll just show up." I hoped someone behind the desk would be understanding to the situation and work us in quickly. I started breathing a little faster. I knew we were going to have to take some action to make Charlie right again.

He dressed and threw his bundled-up dirty clothes in the washing machine. He didn't want me to see the blood.

"You better put a towel under me in the car."

"Why, is it that bad?"

"I'll mess up your seats."

"We're going in your car, then." I tried to keep it light, but I didn't take the time to grab a towel. And we went in my car.

My heart thumped in my throat all the way up Hillsboro Road.

"I'm going to need a wheelchair to get inside," he said, as we turned in to the clinic and approached the canopy.

"Are you serious?"

"Yes, I'm very sick."

I pulled up, stopped, ran inside, and said in a loud voice to the women at the reception desk, "My husband is in the car, he's very ill, he needs a wheelchair, and I need help getting him in here."

Thank God, one responded quickly. She got a nurse who grabbed a wheelchair and took Charlie straight through the waiting room, and the doctor saw him immediately.

"It felt like somebody jabbed a broom handle down my throat." Charlie tilted his head back, his mouth wide open, arms up and bent at the elbows, one fist above the other, as though he was gripping a broom handle. He punched it in downward jabs like one end was in his mouth. He illustrated to the doctor what had happened at three this morning. It was now two in the afternoon.

Oh dear God. I let my head bump back against the wall and said a quick "please take care of him." He hadn't described it this way to me. If only he had. Static filled my head and crackled. It felt like all my wiring came loose, and the wires were flapping, sparks flying, shocks shooting out.

The doctor wasted no time writing up orders for the hospital and alerting a specialist. Charlie was bleeding internally and would need surgery.

Many months later I would come across a bit of information that had meaning at the time, but on this Friday afternoon in a Franklin clinic, I wasn't aware. Major organs could only survive twelve hours without oxygen. It had been eleven.

I wheeled Charlie out to the car, opened the door, and waited for him to get in. He tried to stand up and couldn't. I held his arm to support him and tried to lift him. He was shaking, seizing.

"Stay with me, Charlie! Don't you dare leave me."

I ran back in. "I need help!" The woman who checked us in immediately jumped into action and sent a doctor and nurse outside. "Call 9-1-1," I said. They wheeled Charlie back in, running, and threw him on a table and held his legs up, and I helped hold them, and it was like a Code Blue with every doctor in the clinic working on him. They put him on a drip and readied him for the ambulance that arrived at the back door. I eased out into the hallway, and an older woman, the wife of the patient in the adjoining exam room, came and stood with me. Then I ran to my car and watched the ambulance speed off in a mix of red lights and siren. I called my sons and my friend Currie. I went by our house and took our little dog, Chaeli, out because I knew I might be at the hospital until late that night. And the EMTs had told me not to try and follow the ambulance.

When I arrived at the emergency room of the Franklin hospital, Charlie was lying on a gurney, naked, covered up with a sheet. He was writhing, kicking off the cover, pulling out wires, and yelling with pain. The ER doctor gave him blood and told me he couldn't get a blood pressure reading except by Doppler. I kept trying to comfort Charlie and cover him, but it was getting scary.

Then Currie showed up. "I couldn't let you be here by yourself."

"It's bad, isn't it?" Charlie asked, moaning.

"You're going to have some surgery," I said, pulling the sheet over this leg, then that one.

"Oooooh, there goes my business."

I stepped out in the hallway and called Charlie's brother in Huntingdon, two hours away.

"David, I've got Charlie in the emergency room. He's going to have surgery."

"I'll be there . . . it may be tomorrow morning."

"I-I don't know if he'll be here tomorrow morning." I don't know why I said that.

"I gotcha. I'm on my way."

They finally moved Charlie out of emergency and then called me back.

The specialist, a gastroenterologist, said "I'm not the one who can fix him. They've called in the best vascular surgeon in the area. He had just left the hospital with out-of-town plans, but agreed to come back in and do surgery." He put his arm around me, and we stood there outside the room where Charlie was and looked at him through the glass.

The vascular surgeon arrived and stood by the bed as Charlie cried and twisted.

"I've been here for days, and they won't give me anything for the pain."

"I'm going to take care of that. I'm going to give you something." The doctor spoke in a compassionate voice and assured Charlie he would address his most immediate need.

I thought Charlie was exercising his wry humor when he said he'd been here for days, but perhaps he really thought he had. Either way, those would be his last words. He was put into a coma-like state, completely paralyzed, taken to surgery, and I was sent to the waiting room.

My friend Colleen called and said she was coming to the hospital to sit with Currie and me. She'd had a hysterectomy three days earlier.

"No," I told her. "You can't drive yet. Don't come." Currie told her the same thing.

"I'll get a ride, I'll come if I want to. Y'all should just shut up about it and don't try to boss me around," she said in her smilingly adamant voice.

She arrived a half hour later. All three of us had had hysterectomies by different doctors in the last six months. Currie's was first, mine was in April, and now, Colleen, in June. No one else was in the waiting room, so we lifted our shirts, unzipped our pants, and compared scars. Mine was the neatest.

A nurse came out during Charlie's surgery to give a progress report. He had an occlusion in the mesenteric artery. The surgeon had opened the artery and removed the clots. The clots had infarcted Charlie's bowels. An infarction is when the tissue dies due to insufficient supply of blood and lack of oxygen.

Currie and Colleen said they were going to get a glass of iced tea. We all catered to Colleen's passion for tea. She kept a glass with her at all times. I suspected my friends wanted to talk about my situation, too. They left my side for about fifteen minutes.

The waiting room was narrow and deep and dimly lit, and empty chairs lined the walls. I had chosen a spot in the far back where there were big windows. I sat there trying to squelch the panic, yet still unaware of how critical my husband was.

The silhouette of a woman about my age appeared in the backlit doorway. She entered and walked with a mission, and she was aimed right for me. I couldn't believe she would come all the way back where I was and sit. But she did. She chose a chair stuck squat up next to mine and took a seat, her right shoulder one inch from my left. I frowned and folded my arms across my chest. I eyed twenty silent chairs up one side of the room and twenty up the other. I wanted to ask her why she was sitting so close to me.

"Why are you here?" she said.

"My husband is having emergency exploratory surgery." At that point, I did not understand what all was wrong with Charlie. I didn't know why he had a blockage in his artery.

Then she forced her story on me. She was there to visit her husband, who was in intensive care. He'd be going home in a few days. The previous Sunday he had ventured out to play golf. On the way, he fell asleep, ran off the road, and hit a concrete bridge abutment. His car had OnStar, and 9-1-1 was alerted. Paramedics rushed him to the hospital. Emergency room doctors checked him over, and a CT scan was ordered to rule out hidden injuries. Doctors discovered an aneurysm that was leaking between the layers. It had nothing to do with the accident. But it would have killed him within hours or days . . . had he not hit the concrete . . . had his car not had OnStar . . . had the doctors not ordered a CT. She was ecstatic that God had worked everything together to save his life.

Call it divine intervention, call it a miracle, or call it luck.

Currie and Colleen came back into the room. The woman got up. "Blessings to your husband," she said, and she left.

"She blessed your husband," Colleen said with a questioning nod of her head. "He's going to be okay."

She gave Colleen a reason to believe that things would turn around and be all right, and she gave me that, too. It was a sign from God. Surely, God had sent her as a messenger to bring comfort to me. Why else would she have come straight to me?

A few hours later I would learn that my husband also had an aneurysm that leaked between the layers. Only he had no early CT, no early diagnosis, no divine intervention, no miracle, no luck.

That woman had squeezed hope all over me like honey. People should be careful and not throw their miracles around because God doesn't give miracles to everybody.

My brother-in-law arrived. David had called a cousin who lived in Franklin, and Linda and John came to wait with us. Everybody left about ten, except David. My son Todd and his wife arrived from Mississippi about midnight, after Currie had called and told them it was serious, and they should head home.

The family was called back to see Charlie. Tubes were running all over and around him. Blood was running through the tubes, along with bits of brown solid material.

"What's that?" Todd asked the nurse.

"Blood and bile."

"Wuh . . . is he . . . bleeding out?"

"Yes."

I stepped away from the bed and faced the wall. I frowned, gave my head a shake, trying to startle myself into awareness. I could lose my husband.

I never believed it would happen. Bad things never happened to me. I'd had an easy life.

Later I stood against the concrete wall of the hallway, and the doctor explained that Charlie's organs had been without oxygen and weren't functioning normally. Maybe his brain, too. I couldn't take the thought of this brilliant mind being compromised. I had fallen in love with that brain—the brain with an electrical engineering degree from the University of Tennessee and an MBA from the University of Pittsburgh. The brain that knew how to install extra electrical outlets in our house and could work a whole crossword puzzle in ten minutes. I rammed my head back against the wall as hard as I could.

"Is he retired?" the doctor asked.

The question hit me like cold water. If Charlie was retired and thus useless to society, were they just going to let him die? I didn't know. I growled an answer with all the viciousness I could summon, and I shook a finger like an old schoolteacher, fussing.

"NO. He owns a business, he has companies all over Nashville depending on him to keep their computers and networks up and running, he's got to be at work on Monday. FIX HIM."

About two in the morning, after more attempts to assess and treat, the surgeon walked through the door of the waiting room, straight over to our little family of four, picked up a straight chair, turned it around, and sat down on it like I used to do as a child when I was pretending I was riding a horse.

Charlie had had an aortic dissection, complete, from throat to groin.

Aortic dissection: A condition in which a tear develops in the inner layer of the aorta, the large blood vessel that branches off the heart. Blood surges through the tear into the middle layer of the aorta, causing the inner and middle layers to separate, or dissect. If the blood-filled channel ruptures through the outside aortic wall, aortic dissection is often fatal.

That process had begun at three in the morning—what he had described to our primary physician with the broom handle illustration. An aneurysm in his aorta had leaked for days between the layers and finally there was a rupture, and the inner layer of his aorta had blown away, all the way down the pipe, causing artery occlusion, shutting off blood flow to major organs.

"He has a five percent chance of survival without divine intervention, and that's only if we can get him to Vanderbilt."

I sat there, letting his words catch up with my inability to think and process in the shock of the night. I heard a whirring sound, the chopping of air, the beating of blades outside the big windows behind me. I knew that sound.

"How will he get there?"

"Ambulance, I guess."

I looked him in the eyes, then turned my head to the window—the noise was louder, the sky black, the parking lot lamps shining on cars, and the blinking lights and movement of LifeFlight rushing to the ground. Then I looked back at the doctor.

"Weh, uh, I guess they sent the helicopter," he said.

"Five percent chance?" David asked.

"Maybe six, but that's all I'd give him."

We went to where Charlie was and stood outside his room while the LifeFlight team prepared him for the trip to Nashville. I heard questioning coming from the room. *When was the CT done? Why . . . ?* We were hanging by a thread at this point. I wanted the doctors and nurses to hush, hurry, and get Charlie out of here and to a place where he had a chance.

The team rolled Charlie out, and he was piled high with monitors and tubes and all kinds of stuff, and it was the worst thing I'd ever seen in my whole entire life, and they all went into the elevator. The hospital staff lined the hallway. It was quiet, solemn, they knew what was happening, I didn't, and I just stood there not knowing what to do. The head of the flight squad pointed out a spot in the elevator to me and said, "Ma'am, you come stand right here by your husband." I rode the elevator down, then the head guy gave me instructions about where I should go at Vanderbilt University Medical Center. They rushed my husband away, and all I could think was that the next place would fix him.

Our family of four arrived at Todd's Murano in the parking lot as the helicopter revved up and lifted, turned, and headed north, following Interstate 65 from Franklin to Nashville.

"I've done this too many times," I cried. The first time was when Dad had his heart attack in the mid-eighties and was flown out of his Mississippi Delta town of Cleveland to Memphis and Baptist Memorial.

"I know," Todd said. He was twelve back then.

I opened the back door and heard him say to his wife, "Tell me this isn't happening."

Death Comes

June 28, 2008

A giant sucking force was in place, pulling everything toward an end, like water in a bathtub circling fast, going down. I couldn't do anything about it, but sit there weak-armed and weak-legged and tremble.

We were in a big waiting room at Vanderbilt. Cory was with us now. The room was sectioned off in chair groupings for families, all waiting for news on loved ones. Charlie was in his second surgery. The staff had already told me they couldn't pink him up and they were having a hard time getting him off the heart-lung machine.

For thirty-eight hours nurses and doctors at two hospitals kept asking me if there was anything I needed, anything I wanted. I just needed them to fix my husband, and I just wanted to take my husband home with me, where we could get back to our lives. I wanted to be out of here and normal again. How could we ever get back to normal after what he'd suffered?

The first doctor who operated had made it clear that without divine intervention, Charlie only had a five percent chance of survival. Todd, Cory, and I had already been to the chapel, where we cried and prayed out loud, asking God to step in and do something—to perform a miracle. "Our little family has been through so much," Cory said, and his crying grew to a wail. The three of us were left in a heap together the day my first husband, their father, moved out in 1994, but we pulled ourselves up, went out to eat at Garfield's, Cory's favorite Green Hills restaurant, the

one we always went to after his swim meets at the Sportsplex, and
we vowed to be okay because we had each other. Months after that,
the two sons were the only ones present by my side at my wedding
to Charlie. Now I had these two young men who cried with me and
stood strong on each side of me. It was not my nature to let them
do that. But I yielded.

In the noise of a hundred people or more in the waiting room, it
came to me that there was something I needed, wanted, and should
ask for. I looked at Todd and pushed out the words.

"Everybody's been asking me, and there is something I want."

"Okay, what?"

"If my husband isn't going to make it, I want to see him one last
time." I shook my finger in the air, landing on *one* and *last* and *time*. I
could feel the emotion spitting out in the staccato of my words, and
I could feel the furrows in my forehead crunching hard together.

"Okay. I'll let them know." He turned and walked over to the
nurses' glassed-in office and called one out and told her my request.
He could always talk anybody into anything.

I didn't know why I asked for that. Thoughts were coming to me
like sparks being thrown from a misfire. I was in a buzz. Nothing
was right. But I somehow understood that once Charlie left the
hospital, he'd be gone, cremated, and I'd never get to touch him
again, kiss him, see him in life or still close to life. This was a big
thing, and I wanted it.

The surgeon came in and reported that they were still having
problems getting Charlie off the heart-lung machine. They would
take him off and he'd be fine for forty-five minutes, then he'd crash.

"There's still one more surgery we can do. I think the outcome
will be the same, but I've got a team ready if you want us to go ahead
with it." He took a few steps back away from the family.

It was a Hail Mary.

"Oh, God, what am I going to do? Charlie wouldn't want all
this." I rested my forehead in my hand, and my head was full with
the decision I had to make.

I looked up at Todd and searched his face for answers. Nothing. It was my call. "I have to give him every chance to live."

"Okay, then that's it, we'll tell the doctor."

I looked over at the surgeon, who had one arm crossed over his chest, the other elbow resting on it, his fist over his mouth, and he stepped closer.

"I can't walk away from this place without giving him every chance to survive. Do it. Do everything you can."

How many times over the years had Charlie and I talked about such an instance? "I want to go quickly," he'd say. "Don't let me linger. If I'm irreversibly ill, if I cannot be whole again, let me die. No heroics. I don't want to be less than what I am now." I'd always respond, "You need to know if I think there's a chance for you to survive, I will take it. I will give you every opportunity to live." He'd always argue back. "I don't want to linger. If I do, go to the Hemlock Society website and find a way to end my life." I'd say, "I could never do that." He'd say, "I would want you to." Now, we were playing it out in real life.

This was madness.

The surgeon nodded and shuffled a bit and said he understood that we had made a special request to see Charlie one last time. He warned me it was bloody and messy in the OR and I probably did not want to go in there. I told him I did want to go in there. Todd took his elbow and walked him to the door, talking to him.

I was sitting next to Cory, so close that my right arm and his left arm touched from shoulder to elbow. Adrenalin was pumping through me. I could feel the beats in my head and chest, and my shirt over my heart was moving in and out with each thump. Charlie was in his third surgery. The clock was ticking.

Noise in the room was pummeling me, and my body kept trying to choke it out. Other-family conversations swirled, buzzed, heightened, churned the air, and echoed between heads and the ceiling.

I leaned my head back and looked up at the long flat ceiling light. Suddenly I felt a warm energy. A quiet, liquid smoothness came at me, into me, sank into my front, began to wrap around me. I could feel it enfolding me, touching against my sides and back until it held me, and I was fully enclosed in the presence. It was the calmest feeling I'd ever known. It was not of this world. It was Charlie. Then I heard his voice. I clearly heard the sound, but I knew it was not out loud, and something nobody else could hear. His words came with an urgency.

"I'm going, I'm going."

I felt complete peace.

I wouldn't grasp what had happened here, though, until hours, maybe days, later. This was death, and my husband found me in that huge medical facility to tell me he was dying and going and leaving me. Charlie had told me fourteen years earlier in the last three lines of the wedding vows he wrote to me, "I cherish you. I want to endure all things with you. I want to walk home to God with you." And he did.

"You stopped shaking," Cory said, looking over at me. "You've been shaking all day, and now you're not. Why aren't you shaking?"

I shrugged and stammered a bit. "I-I don't know."

He was getting a little ragged-nerved because a child in the family behind the cubicle separating our tragedy and theirs was being loud and obnoxious. We were trying to ignore it, but it was ever grating. We hadn't seen Charlie all day, he'd been in surgery, maybe eight, ten hours, I didn't know, I had no concept of time. Cory got up and stepped around the wall. "Can y'all please tone it down a bit? There are people in here dealing with stuff." They toned it down for a minute, but then cranked it back up.

"Leave them alone," I said. "I don't want you getting into an argument."

Todd got up and went to the nurses' station. Maybe they called him over, or maybe he went to ask for a quiet room, some place private because there was too much noise and we couldn't deal with what we were dealing with in the middle of it. A nurse escorted us back into their glassed-in private space and put us in a conference room that no one was using.

Things were happening in light-flashes of significant moments that my memory was storing away. Light-flashes, like the flash of a camera in the snap of a picture. The image is kept. The peripherals of transitions and in-between details would not stay intact.

I plopped my purse down on a long mahogany conference table and sat down at one end of it. Cory sat next to me. Todd stood and paced, while his wife sat at the table across from me. David had just left to go back to Huntingdon. He'd walked down the hall and found the person assigned to Charlie, once Charlie was moved out of surgery. The nurse had drawn him a diagram that explained aortic dissection and updated him on Charlie's status. "I think I know how this is going to come out," David had told me. "And I've got a much bigger job ahead of me back home. I've got to tell Louise." His mother. Charlie's mother. Eighty-seven. In a nursing home. How do you tell a woman she has outlived her firstborn son? Her second-born, who took life responsibilities seriously, was torn between a mother, a brother, and the brother's soon-to-be widow. Widow. I hated that word. I never thought I would be a widow in my fifties. "If it happens," David had said, "don't call me. I don't want to know yet. I've got to prepare Louise. I need to be able to tell her the truth, that Charles is ill and might not survive. I need to ease her into it."

Fifteen minutes or thirty minutes went by. The door opened. The surgeon rushed in.

"We're losing ground. If you still want to say goodbye, we need to go right now."

Losing ground? Erratic and irrational thoughts darted about. It didn't matter—I could not have processed them if they had been rational. My body went heavy, like lead. I looked at Todd. "You going?"

"I'll walk down with you, but I'm not going in."

"I'm not going," Cory said.

"Let's go," the doctor said.

We were losing ground. I got up. Followed. Ran behind him. Down two, maybe three, or five, flights of stairs. Not knowing where I was going or what I'd get into when I got there. The surgeon was a flight ahead. Taking the stairs two or three at a time. Todd was at my elbow, there to catch me if I fell. I couldn't keep up. I couldn't run down stairs that fast. Why was the doctor going so fast? Why was he running? Why was he making me run?

"Would you want an autopsy?"

"No." Why was he asking me this?

"What about organs . . . well, there aren't any organs we can use . . ." His voice trailed off.

Wait, what? No organs good enough? I'd want him all together anyway. I didn't think he'd volunteered to be an organ donor.

The surgeon stopped outside a set of doors. "You won't get to see his face, but you can say your peace."

"Will I be alone with my husband?"

"There's a team of twelve in there. C'mon." He reached out for my hand.

He led me into the operating room, where my husband was, where he'd spent most of the day. It was bright, and there were red, yellow, and blue tubes like coiled wire that ran along the walls and looped around each other and filled the room. I didn't know what they were. Doctors in blue scrubs stood randomly away from the surgery table, hands clasped behind them, in front of them, heads bowed. It didn't register with me that no one was working on Charlie. They were just standing still. I saw someone reach down and grab up something off the floor—plastic, maybe wrapping from something they'd used on Charlie. I decided not to look around, just to look down at the floor, which was not like me, because I usually wanted to take in all the details, but I didn't understand what was in here, and I might see something I didn't want to.

Charlie was lying there, covered in blue, with a screen separating his head from the surgical field. His head was covered. The surgeon led me to a small round stool with wheels and told me to push up to the table and talk to my husband. I sat down. I tried to push the stool forward with my feet. It wouldn't go, and I looked up at the surgeon. He reached down, grabbed the padded seat, and pulled me up to the top end of the table, behind Charlie's head.

Black curls. That's all I could see. I looked at those curls, memorized them, and tried to think of something to say. Were these the final words I'd ever say to him? I knew that, I didn't know that, I could not understand the significance of the moment.

"You're the best thing that ever happened to me. You're the best thing that ever happened to my family." I said some more things, I don't remember what they were, and then it came to me what he'd always told me that he wanted people to remember and say about him and his life. *Charlie Rhodes. He was a pretty good man.*

I stumbled with it. "Hey, you were a pretty good guy."

I leaned over and kissed the black curls. With my nose in his hair, I breathed in. I knew it would be the last time. I didn't know it would be the last time. I got up off the stool. The surgeon pushed a switch. The machinery fell silent. He reached for me. Put his arm around me. Walked me to the door.

"He passed when you were talking to him."

"Are you serious?"

How could that be? How could it happen that way?

It was a soft and gentle way for him to tell me.

Later, it would hit me that I knew the exact moment of death, and that wasn't it. Charlie had come to me himself and told me he was going.

Much later, I would realize that even though I didn't comprehend that my husband was dead there on the table in the OR, this was a powerful beginning to healing. The surgeon let me come into the holy realm where the team had fought a battle to win a life, to save Charlie. In the chaos that death brought to life, I was allowed to close out their efforts. To connect with the spirit, to say goodbye. To see, to touch the flesh, to give one last kiss before Charlie was taken away. To ease that spirit beside me in another realm.

Four years later, Todd would confess, "I've never told you this before. When I told the surgeon you wanted to see Charlie one last time, he looked hard at me and said that it would happen very quickly, and there wouldn't be a lot of time. I told him that was okay, that the important thing was for you to say goodbye, to have closure. I said 'I'm asking you to do whatever needs to be done to make that happen.' In my mind I was thinking, 'If you have to stage a final farewell, please do so.' He held my gaze for a good five seconds, then nodded, and said okay, that he was going to have the nurse move us into a conference room that connected to the stairwell, that he didn't know how long it would take, but you needed to be ready."

The surgeon walked me out the door where Todd waited and then walked with us to the elevator. "We were actually able to repair the heart. His other organs were too long without oxygen." The major artery blockage caused by the dissection had done too much damage.

Primary cause of death: Intestinal Ischemia. Secondary: Type A Aortic Dissection.

Charlie didn't go to the hospital soon enough.

Todd and I got on the elevator. A woman with pink balloons stepped in. "Was there a baby born?" I asked. "Yes," she said.

The irony hit me. One leaves, one comes.

All my life, I'd wondered how I could ever walk away and leave my loved one in a hospital morgue. I'd always told myself I wouldn't leave. I would stay right there with his body, outside the door, if need be, and go with the body as it was transported to the funeral home. Now, I realized I was leaving. I walked out the hospital's front doors, into the sunlight, breathing in hot air, in the noise and bustle of the city, with people moving fast in the business of life.

How could life keep going on all around me?

It was my moment for life to stop.

I got in the car with Todd to go home. The other two followed. I don't think I cried. This must have been shock.

I was picked up out of my happy life and thrown down on a hard road to go on a journey I didn't plan to take. I wasn't packed for it, I didn't have tickets to anywhere, I didn't have a map. I didn't want to take this trip. I didn't have a choice. I had to go.

Wedding Vows

Written by Charlie Rhodes, December 31, 1994

I open my heart to tender caring,
>   Giving, sharing, trusting, yielding.
I promise not to question your needs.
I promise to seek your peace.
I promise to put your happiness first.
I promise to love you with all that I have,
>   All that I am, all that I can and will become.
>   For all time.
For it is in giving that I receive. And it is in helping you awake that I awaken.
I cherish you.
I want to endure all things with you.
I want to walk home to God with you.

Our hearts entwined, existence defined,
A new journey begins.

The First Week

June 28, Saturday, the evening of

The trip home seemed long—down Hillsboro Road from Vanderbilt in Nashville, through tight Hillsboro Village, busy Green Hills with its mall and restaurant traffic, the rich quietness of Forest Hills, to Old Hickory Boulevard, then south into Williamson County, to Franklin. I'd driven this pike for twenty years and loved every inch of it—the rolling hills, green pastures, the old red barn with a big flag hanging on it since Nine Eleven, black cows, and tea-colored creeks coiled in distant tree lines running to the Harpeth River. Now, it was just odd how this road could connect death to what was home and a happy life. How this road was taking me to someplace new and different.

I rode in the front passenger seat, with Todd driving. We didn't talk. I glanced over at him to see how he was handling this. Eyes on the road, lips tight, holding it all in. Normal. My phone rang. Linda. Charlie's cousin, who was with us at the Franklin hospital twenty-four hours earlier.

"How's Charles?"

"He just passed away. I'm on the way home."

Passed away. I said that to soften it for her. I don't use that euphemism. Passed. Away. My husband wouldn't have passed away to somewhere else and left me. Passed, an active verb. It sounded like he had a choice of whether or not to pass. He didn't. He died.

I felt glazed. Like the brakes on the car one time when I was a little girl and my daddy drove the family down Lookout Mountain in Chattanooga. The brakes weren't "catching," or slowing and stopping, so Dad had to pull off the road and let them cool. Thoughts like live wires zapped through my head, and emotions were packed inside me, but they weren't "catching" hold to or penetrating the raw place that was my heart. I just couldn't take it all in.

My husband was dead.

By the time we pulled up in front of my house, one thing was weighing on my mind—a story Charlie had written two months earlier about a Styrofoam cup. That little cup had been thrown out of somebody's car window in the middle of busy Trousdale Avenue in front of Charlie's office. He'd watched as the wind of traffic pushed it forward, backward, in arcs, as it dodged heavy tires of behemoth machines with drivers caught up in their own chaos of business, not caring if they smashed the fragile cup into the pavement. As publisher and editor of an online literary magazine, Muscadine Lines: A Southern Journal, I had accepted that story for publication, scheduled for July 1, two days away. I felt a gentle push, an immediacy, to go read the story again right now. I opened the front door, shot straight up the stairs to my office, pulled it up on the computer, and searched it line by line, desperate for connection to my husband and the meaning of his words. The story told of the cup's struggle for survival and how it finally found its resting place. That same gentle push told me there was a message in this story for me because behemoths were all around, squashing the breath out of me. That same gentle push told me I needed to use this story in the funeral service. That same gentle push was Charlie. His spirit. With me.

Next, I went to the dog. Charlie had loved to brag that he lived with two blondes—me and the dog. We'd gotten Chaeli six weeks after my golden retriever died. I found an ad in the paper for a cocker spaniel litter with a buff female in Nashville, and we drove up to the Fairgrounds area to Dottie's kennel to look. Charlie picked up the puppy first, held her in front of his face, and talked to her, then handed me the yellow butterball with curly ears, a freckled face, a white spot on her head, and a white diamond on her neck.

"Is she what you want?" He wrote a check, and that first day with our little Chaeli Foster, Charlie became the Alpha. I was always just a littermate.

I sat down on the bathroom floor with Chaeli, opened the drawstring on the hospital's white plastic bag of belongings, and pulled out Charlie's yellow shirt with blue stripes. They'd cut it off him in the ambulance, thus it was scissor-ripped up the back and covered with blood. I held it under Chaeli's nose and let her smell it, believing she would instinctively know something catastrophic had happened. I held her, hugged her close, and buried my face in her hair. "Daddy's gone. He won't be coming home any more. It's just you and me now." Just the littermates. No Alpha.

My head was filled with a hum. My heart pounded. I could hear it, feel it in my ears. I don't think I cried, though. There was a barrier around me. This was what they called shock. I'd heard about it all my life. Shock was the body's way of protecting a person from pain that was too great to bear at one time—nature's way of softening the blow. I was like a robot, able to go through the motions of life without feeling the pain of the loss. Snippets of a new reality would be shot at me, then go away. My neighbor Vicki came over to pay her respects and brought a big basket of individually wrapped breath mints and small packages of Kleenexes. I didn't need a Kleenex yet. Because I was in shock.

My husband was dead.

About nine, my sister and mother arrived. Todd had called Judi earlier that afternoon and told her she needed to go get Mamaw and head this way—to come on, come now. I met them on the front porch, and we hugged and went into my all-lighted-up living room. My mother was eighty-seven, showing some signs of dementia, and not quite able to process the full impact of what had just happened. My sister sighed deeply and said, "Well. You're just going to have to build a whole new life."

Her words slapped against me and stung, then bounced off my head and echoed. *You're going to have to build a whole new life, you're going to have to build a whole new life, you're going to have to build a whole new life.* The words didn't feel right, and I couldn't let them in. My first reaction was to hit her. But I didn't. I just stood there. Frozen. I didn't want a whole new life. I wanted my old life. I wasn't ready for the old one to end. I wanted my husband. I wanted him to be at home with me. Not them.

"You've done it before," she said. "You can do it again." She was talking about when my first husband left me. I did build a new life then. Met Charlie, married, moved to a new house, got active in the writing community, wrote and edited books, got rid of that old surname I had no business using anymore.

Judi had been a teacher for thirty-two years. She was used to barking out imperatives, helpful advice, and blunt reality. But even in my state of shock, I reeled at the thought of a brand new life.

My husband was dead. He was no longer with me. No longer in our home. In Franklin. At GENISYS. He'd struggled, then found a new resting place. He was the cup he'd written about in that story.

In the days to come, I would learn how to put one heavy foot in front of the other and push myself down that new roadway cut into life, getting blown and knocked about by behemoths, struggling to survive. I, too, was the cup Charlie had written about.

June 29, Sunday, the day after

I'd just inherited a business. That was one of the scariest thoughts that came over me after Charlie died. He'd founded GENISYS Systems Group in 1989 to build computers and provide service for small-to-medium-sized businesses in the greater Nashville area. At one time he had four full-time employees, as well as additional associates. These last two years it was just the two of us. He made service calls and did bench work, and I kept the books. I knew the financial side of the business. I did not know how to fix computers and networks.

This morning at 9:13, I got an email from another business owner in town, a 1997 start-up company with a name similar to ours. In fact, they bought the same domain name in the dot net version. But everybody gravitates to dot com, and so there had been confusion with their customers and vendors as to their contact information. We were getting some of their emails. The owner had repeatedly tried to buy our domain name, and Charlie had refused every time. The owner of that company didn't know that Charlie had died eighteen hours earlier when he sent me an email. Or maybe . . . it was yet another gentle push by Charlie's spirit that prompted the inquiry.

Good Morning,

I thought I would check with you again to see if you have any interest in selling your domain name. Please let me know if you do.

Thank you.

A tingling went up my face, then heat came down. I didn't respond to the email, but I didn't delete it either. Two years later I would reply, negotiate a price with the owner, and let the name go. But in the meantime, I hung on to it.

For now, I had to hold on to Charlie's things. Because if I still had his things, I'd still have part of him. Things took on a life of their own. The bucking bronco cup on his desk three-quarters filled with coffee became significant because his mouth had touched it, and I told everyone to leave it alone and not empty it. The brass Pocket Change tray beside the bed was something he'd touched every day and dropped coins from his pocket there. His slippers—maybe I should wear them. His comb—it still had a hair on it. His hearing aids—he had new ones, five thousand dollars. I had one of them, but where was the other? Was it still in his ear? I had to find it.

Today, I had to make funeral arrangements. The funeral director had called to set up an appointment after Vanderbilt alerted them to come get Charlie. We sat around a conference table at the funeral home in Franklin—me, Todd, Cory, Mark, and Tonja. Mark was Charlie's son, who flew in from Texas with his wife Tonja, but didn't make it before Charlie died. We planned cremation, visitation, and the service.

I knew exactly what to do. It hit me how odd that was, how easy. I realized just how much Charlie and I had talked about death. Most couples don't spend a lot of time discussing end-of-life issues, but Charlie and I did, and he was explicit as to what his wishes were and how he wanted things handled and who would get what. He wanted cremation with no embalming. He wanted some of his ashes scattered in the Tennessee River across from Neyland Stadium in Knoxville and then some with his parents in a Huntingdon cemetery. It served us well for having laid all our wishes on the table.

I had to answer questions for the death certificate. Where was Charlie born? I couldn't remember for sure. I was in the hum that sets in after trauma. I couldn't pick even the simplest answers out of my brain. I knew full well he was born in Huntingdon, Tennessee, in a gas station that had been converted to a house. I'd always teased him about having so many allergies as an adult because he was exposed to petroleum residue as a baby.

Grief keeps you from thinking clearly, from remembering things. That constant buzz in your head covers up stored information. It's a white noise, a rushing sound, like a fast-moving creek, one that you might be sitting beside, only you're not sitting beside it, it's inside you, it's running through your head, and you can't get away from it. It never stops.

Who would do the service? I wanted something meaningful, and as my dad always said, "If you want something done right, do it yourself." So I asked Todd if he'd lead the service. He was an ordained minister—not a practicing one, but during his college days, he'd considered the pastorate as a vocation. No, he said, he couldn't do it. He was too close to Charlie. He didn't think he could keep himself together. Okay, I told him, but think about it. In our family, we take care of our own. And he agreed to do it.

The funeral director told us that Charlie had to be sent off for cremation and might not make it back in time for the service. That piece of information got lost in the buzz inside my head.

The kids and I spent the afternoon at home getting things together to display at visitation. We dug pictures of Charlie out of storage boxes or pulled them up on the computer, printed, and framed them all. I gathered up his Eagle Scout award, some tokens from his years at Alcoa, and his GENISYS car tag. We selected music for the service, and the sons went out to buy CDs of the songs.

I wrote an obituary and emailed it to the funeral home. It would go in _The Tennessean_ newspaper the following day.

June 30, Monday

There's something about seeing it in print. The thwack of the paper on the driveway brought reality home. It's real, it's final, he's really gone. I can't go back.

RHODES, Mr. Charles E. "Charlie," of Franklin passed away Saturday, June 28, 2008 after a brief illness. Graduate of the University of Tennessee and the University of Pittsburgh and had a twenty-year career with Alcoa in Pittsburgh and a twenty-year career as owner and operator of GENISYS Systems Group in Nashville. Preceded in death by father, Stewart Ray Rhodes . . . Memorial services will be conducted 6:00 PM Tuesday, July 1, 2008 with visitation one hour prior to the service . . . .

It cost $296.80 to put the obit in the Nashville paper. I never knew people paid for that. That's why the sentences were clipped— to save lines and money.

That buzz. Filled my head. Was becoming too familiar.

I walked into the open kitchen where my mother, sister, two sons, and a daughter-in-law were all sitting around drinking coffee. They got quiet and looked up at me.

"I've got to go to work." I didn't know I was going to say that. It just came out.

"Okay," Todd said, "I'll go with you."

"The obituary is in the paper. Our customers will see it. I need to go to the office and send out a mass email announcement to let everybody know Charlie died. Then I need to find somebody who can help if our customers have problems." I didn't know I was going to say that either.

"I'll help you," Todd said. "I've done this for a customer in a similar situation."

I didn't have time to sit down and mourn the loss of my husband. I had to take care of business. I had to be Charlie's feet and hands and brain and voice. I had to do what he'd want me to do. He had customers who depended on him. Now, it was my responsibility, and I had to find a way to carry on. I was the business owner, and I would come to see that he was right there beside me, in spirit, unseen, coaxing me on matters that needed to be addressed.

Charlie's four Rules of Life were: "Show up. Be on time. Be fair. Play by the rules." Even in death he needed to show up. Things break. Computers die. Networks go down. He wouldn't want his customers left in the lurch. I couldn't set up a network, diagnose a failed fan, replace a motherboard, consult on a backup plan, or retrieve data from a dead hard drive. I had to have someone to fill in, troubleshoot, and fix computers. I called a long-time associate, and I began to live with Charlie's cell phone twenty-four/seven. My job was to take care of GENISYS customers the way Charlie would have.

And my job was also to find a merger solution for the business.

I was a practical person. A practical person living in the hum that comes with shock and grief, doing things that might not seem appropriate to others. I was a practical person who not only kept the company books, but took care of our personal finances, as well. I had bills to pay, due now, and no income. What was I going to do? How would I survive? Savings? Life insurance?

The reality of bills and money towered over me like a threatening behemoth. I knew I had to minimize the outgoing because there was no incoming, so I began snatching out of the air random Death Duties that would cancel or combine bills. I called my car insurance agent and transferred Charlie's car to my policy, then canceled his. The whole time we were married we had separate insurances. During our first few years, Charlie had four minor accidents. He backed into a sign post that was at least a hundred feet high, he backed into a little sports car at Donut Den, he ran into the back of a car that bumped into a school bus and he didn't even have his driver's license with him, and then he pulled out in front of a car as he was leaving our street. He told me the car that hit him had to be going at least fifty in a thirty, but I knew exactly what had happened: he looked for coming traffic, didn't see any, took a sip of coffee, pulled up his socks one at a time, then proceeded without looking again, and wham. I told him he wasn't getting on my policy ever—my rates would go up. We laughed and kept it that way.

Somewhere in some isolated corner of my mind, I understood that with the loss of my husband came the loss of all sources of income, eventually the business, and ultimately, I'd have to give up our house. I couldn't afford to stay there.

Now, my responsibility as publisher and editor of Muscadine Lines: A Southern Journal weighed on me, and I put the finishing touches on the July-September issue and uploaded it. Charlie's story about the Styrofoam cup, "A Will to Live," went live.

July 1, Tuesday

We went early and set up the display tables for visitation. I assigned the girls of the family—nieces Hayley and Chaderlee, daughter-in-law, and Cory's new girlfriend—the task of decorating and setting out the significant mementos and pictures of Charlie's life. It was the first time I'd met Leah since she and Cory had gotten together at an Obama rally two months earlier. It was good for me to delegate. I needed to learn that other people can take care of your business and do a good job.

People came. Family. Cousins. Neighbors. My friends in the writing community—the Williamson County Council for the Written Word and the Tennessee Writers Alliance. Nearly all Charlie's customers. Even his doctor. It surprised me because we had always told each other we wouldn't have anyone at our funerals because we didn't have friends. We stayed to ourselves, worked, didn't entertain, didn't spend time with others, except for an occasional dinner with our Geezer Group of four cousins and their spouses, all present tonight, and an occasional lunch Charlie had with his ROMEO group (Retired Old Men [from Alcoa] Eating Out), present, as well.

A table at the front of the chapel held a large flower arrangement in University of Tennessee orange and white, a picture of Charlie at Volunteer stadium during a football game, his orange Vols cap, and a wooden urn with a ceramic Vols fan—wearing a white shirt with an orange T on it, an orange cap, and sunglasses—seated on top of the container that was supposed to hold Charlie's ashes.

Charlie was not in there. His top two Rules of Life were "Show up" and "Be on time," but he didn't make it to his own funeral in time.

Shortly after visitation began, however, the funeral director came to me and quietly told me he'd just arrived—"He's in the building," she said—and asked if I thought it would be too intrusive, with all the people standing around, to remove the vessel, put his ashes in it, and return it to the table. I told her we'd leave it as it was. She pressed in my palm a keepsake charm I'd ordered with a small amount of ashes inside, closed my fingers around it, and said, "Here, hold this during the service. You'll have him with you."

I sat on the front row next to Cory. His arm was wrapped tightly around my shoulder. My best friends, Susie, Colleen, and Currie, sat behind me. I listened to the words put together by my older son.

"About fourteen years ago," Todd began, "my mom said she was having dinner with a man named Charlie who had been working on her office computer network. That dinner led to a second date. That date to another, and soon the weeks became months. And then one day in late December, my brother and I found ourselves standing as best men in the wedding of our mother to Charlie Rhodes.

"At some point before the wedding date, Charlie came to me in that straightforward and unassuming manner of his and said that he didn't expect to replace my dad, he didn't expect anything at all . . . except to love and care for Kathy—my mother—and to make a life with her.

"In fourteen years, Charlie never once wavered in that commitment. I grew to know and love and respect Charlie more than just about any other man in my life—as a husband and member of my family, and as a successful businessman.

"The events of the past few days have been a shock, to say the least. No one saw this coming. But it came. And here we are. For our family, today is the first day of moving on. The first of many firsts . . . ."

Then I went to the podium. "Charlie always told me that after all was said and done, all he really wanted was for people to be able to say about him: 'Charlie Rhodes, he was a pretty good guy.' He wished that to be his epitaph.

"He never forgot where he came from—small town, raised by hard-working, church-going parents with Christian values. He was a man of honesty and fairness and integrity. He was the most giving person I have ever known. It was always 'others first.' That included me.

"He had a healthy view of death. It's a natural part of life, he'd say. When it's my time, I'm ready, I'm prepared to go.

"I am blessed and better to have known this man. Charlie Rhodes, he was indeed a pretty good guy."

Todd returned to the podium. "I've been asked to read a story Charlie wrote in the final weeks of his life. This was written, of course, with no knowledge of what was in store—only as an average thought in an average day in Charlie's life.

A Will to Live

Charlie Rhodes, a.k.a. Winston Rand

Trudging through life, coping with the day-to-day challenges and turmoil, we sometimes need a reminder that we too can survive, even beyond all odds. Those little reminders come in various packages. Sometimes it's a child with a serious affliction who is happy and smiling; other times, a warm, frisky puppy that has not a care in the world except to please you; and occasionally, it will be the totally unexpected. Such was the case one day last week.

I arrived back at the office in late afternoon, and something caught my eye as I walked from the car to the office entrance. It took a few seconds for it to register that I was seeing an empty Styrofoam cup in the center turn lane of the busy street out front. There was a push of air from heavy traffic in both directions, causing the little truncated cone to roll in an arc first one way, then the other. The occasional draft of a larger vehicle would move it up and down its chosen lane a few feet. Then more rolling in arcs around its new pivot point until another large draft moved it a few feet forward or backward.

Becoming quickly mesmerized, I stood for perhaps fifteen minutes watching the struggle, the close misses, the movement to and fro. At some point I realized I was cheering the little cup onward in its quest to survive against the impossible odds of the multi-ton monsters bearing down on it from every side. And then it occurred to me how much like life that is. Wishing the dancing traveler well, I went on into the office. Half an hour later after checking email, washing up, and shutting down for the evening, I emerged to find the cup still at it. It had moved about twenty or thirty feet down the turn lane and seemed to be slightly damaged, but not enough to keep it from rolling and arcing, performing its death defying dance. After watching a few more minutes, I had to leave the cup to its unique brand of madness, knowing full well that it would be flattened or completely gone come morning.

Imagine my surprise and delight to arrive back at the office the following day to find the cup, not squashed by one of the many behemoths that passed this way during the night, but intact, resting gently on the grass a few feet from the street. It had a nick, but was otherwise alive and well. I thought of placing the cup back in the middle of the turn lane for another go, but decided it may prefer the resting place it had chosen and worked so hard to reach. Then I was tempted to take it in and leave it sitting on my credenza as a reminder. But such an adventurer needs freedom and would not fare well in captivity. So I left it where it was and carried away the memory of its struggles and the lesson of perseverance it taught.

"Saturday evening upon returning from the hospital, my mom remembered this story and was moved to go and re-read it. Its meaning was immediately clear. We took solace in the thought that, like the cup, Charlie has now found the resting place he has chosen and worked so hard to reach. And I think that maybe we, too, are like the cup, having been tossed and twirled about by the loss of our loved one.

"But as Charlie has left us to our unique brand of madness, my hope is that each of us—in our own way and in our own time—will find a resting place far away from this sorrow."

To close the service, we played "Rocky Top," because no service for Charlie would be complete without a mention of UT football.

Afterward, the funeral home staff delivered to my house the flowers friends had sent in memory of Charlie. The funeral director delivered the Belmont manufactured rosewood urn I'd selected for Charlie's ashes, a smooth contemporary design I knew he'd like. Charlie was now in there. I sat on the couch in the living room, the front door wide open, and watched as they brought in arrangements and placed them on tables. I held Charlie in my lap and felt an odd comfort that he was finally home, yet the hum in my head sounded louder than ever. My body knew it wasn't supposed to be this way. All that was left of Charlie was in one wooden box nine and a half inches high on my lap against the black cotton I wore.

My sister and mother had left for home from the chapel immediately after the service. My two sons, along with a wife and a girlfriend, were still with me. They and the dog and the Belmont urn and the business I'd inherited would form the entirety of my life for the rest of that week.

The funeral was now over, and an end was setting in, after the hubbub of people, guests, friends, family, before getting on with life in some strange and unrecognizable form.

I remembered what Alyce West Richardson, my hometown of Cleveland next-door neighbor of fifty-five years, a widow of twenty years, told my mother after my father died: "You never get over it; you just learn to live with it." I would grow to understand that.

I intuitively knew this journey of learning to "live with it" was one I was starting out on by myself. I'd gone to church and prayed all my life, read my Bible, depended on God, even begged God on occasion for answers and justice and miracles, and now I was facing a time when I would hold my distance. I felt spurned.

When a doctor tells you that your husband has a five percent chance of survival without divine intervention, and you sit in a hospital chapel and cry and pray out loud to God with your sons who are crying, too, your whole world hanging by one thin thread, and God does not step in and change the course of things—well, what do you do with that? I mean, this was significant, this was life, precious life, fragile life, and I was praying desperately for life for my husband, and the answer was no, he could not have life. This set up a struggle in me. How could it not?

God was like the moon shining down. I knew it was up there, there was light around me, I had a dim view of the way, but I couldn't feel any warmth from that light.

I couldn't feel God. The light wasn't touching me.

"God, where are you?"

Silence.

"God, why? Why Charlie? Why me? Why this?"

Silence.

God had always been my pivot point. He was where I'd always placed my stationary foot. I didn't know how to process that God was not carrying me through this, that it seemed he'd abandoned me, and if God was in this, why did he take away my husband? He didn't bless my husband like he did the husband of the woman who'd barged into my personal space at the Franklin hospital. Was I not as good and deserving of a husband as she was?

And who was I to question God?

I was nothing more than an empty Styrofoam cup. A vessel that at one time was filled. Now, a fragile thing that could be crushed and broken to pieces by some giant. Pushed and blown and knocked around by behemoths. At the random mercy of whatever was out there.

I didn't feel anger toward God. It was more like a cold resolve. I believed he'd told me this was mine to handle.

I didn't want to numb my pain with the crutches of supplications. I didn't need the repeated mantras of comfort verses. It seemed these would leave me weak, a victim, on the bottom of the heap, dependent on something or someone to pull me up and out of it. I needed to embrace the pain of loss and work it out of me.

If I was all screwed up theologically and emotionally, then so be it. This wasn't the time I could figure all that out.

My faith knew there was light for the way. I remembered the poem on a Bible bookmark that Minnie Patton White, my Sunday School teacher at First Baptist in my hometown, gave me when I was sixteen and had no understanding of the sorrows and struggles life could bring. It was an old hymn titled "What God Hath Promised" by Annie Johnson Flint. I remembered our class going to Mrs. White's house for tea the Saturday afternoon she gave us the markers, how we dressed up in our Sunday clothes and heels, how we sat there holding our dainty cups and keeping our knees together, and how she was so small and soft and we were gangly and awkward, and how she always tried to give us something to hold on to, and how we loved her for it. "God hath not promised skies always blue, Flower-strewn pathways all our lives through; God hath not promised sun without rain, Joy without sorrow, peace without pain. But God hath promised strength for the day, Rest for the labor, light for the way . . . ."

I'd always believed there must be feet with prayers, and I needed to remember this now. I needed to stand up on what was within me, put one foot in front of the other, walk, move forward, do something, make things happen.

"Yea, though I WALK . . . ." (Psalm 23:4 KJV)

July 2, Wednesday

"Sell the house. Immediately."

That was the advice I got from a trusted friend of Charlie's, who was also a customer of GENISYS. I'd often brought up to Charlie the fact that if he died, I couldn't stay in our house on Wimbledon Circle and make the house payment. The monthly note was too high. Charlie would always counter, try to explain, and then he finally told me that if anything ever happened to him, the first thing I should do was call this friend, who'd tell me how I could manage the house payment and stay put. I'd called Sunday and set up an appointment for today.

"Get an apartment." The friend was looking out for the small reserves Charlie and I had accumulated. He also gave business advice and sent me to interview a computer company that might be interested in merging.

Selling the house: I couldn't do it right now.

Merging the business: I had to take care of GENISYS first.

One thing at a time.

I met with the owner of the Nashville computer company Charlie's friend recommended, toured their office, and observed how they handled technical support. They did troubleshooting remotely. My customers were used to a man on site. The world might be moving in that direction, but not me, not now.

I gave notice to our office complex management that GENISYS would be closing. We'd paid the first and last month's rent when we moved in, which meant I would use the deposit money to cover July and I'd move out at the end of the month.

Other random to-do's from an imaginary list of Death Duties started clicking through my head like ticker tape. I called the mortgage company and put the house in MY name, instead of OUR name. I called the insurance company of one of Charlie's smaller policies—ten thousand dollars. I could live on that until I found a means of income. My sons were still at home to help with the footwork of faxing requests for changes, along with copies of the death certificate the funeral home had provided.

July 3, Thursday

"We're supposed to start the process of in vitro fertilization tomorrow," Todd said. "We can stay here if you need us and put this off until next month. Otherwise, we need to leave for home today."

They'd made a decision to go this route two months earlier. I'd already bought a pink dress, anxious for a granddaughter.

"You go home. You have lives to live."

Life goes on.

On the business front, I interviewed a one-man-show computer company who would service my customers. At least GENISYS could carry on until a permanent solution was found. But it would only carry on for two weeks, when I had a customer with a network down, and the one-man-show went out of town on vacation without a thought about my customer. Charlie's trusted friend referred me to another company that was glad to step in and help out.

July 4, Friday

Cory and Leah headed back to North Carolina. For the first time, I was alone.

The pump on the goldfish pond stopped up and tripped off everything electrical on that circuit. And just where was my electrical-engineer husband? I needed him to fix it. I knew there was a GFCI button I should press, but I couldn't remember where it was. Grief hormones wreak havoc with the memory. The frustration and anguish of loss and of not being able to take care of the simple stuff he used to take care of set in.

I hated that pond.

Charlie didn't want a pond, but the first spring we were in our new house, I was determined to dig a hole by the patio and fill it with water and fish. I saw the end. He saw the means. I told him I'd do all the work—he wouldn't have to do a thing. I hooked Todd into helping. He was in college then, had gotten his first credit card, and it had a big balance. He did the hard manual labor of digging and hauling the dirt to a back corner of the yard for a tiered flower bed in exchange for payment on his account. Charlie couldn't stand it for long, though, and had to get involved to make sure we got the rigid pond liner in correctly, got it level, and got the pump installed properly, seeing that no money was wasted in the process. Then came water irises and lily pads and eleven goldfish and koi.

It was beautiful, and the sound of the trickling waterfall over huge stones, engineered by Charlie, was soothing. But maintaining it was back-breaking work. Every spring we had to drain it, scoop nasty black-sludge decayed matter from the bottom, scrub the sides, rid it of algae, and re-fill it with fresh water.

Now in the heat of summer with no working electricity to the pump to move the water around, that pond would just sit still and breed mosquitoes and grow algae like mad. I didn't care.

I didn't care that it was July the Fourth either. There would be no homemade ice cream or thick steaks injected with marinade or flags waving from flower pots at my house. Charlie and I had planned to go to a party at Gloria and Jim's house with the Geezer Group cousins, so now I had to go without him.

Linda and John gave me a ride. Gloria's house was filled with red, white, and blue, little flags everywhere, lots of food, memories shared, laughs, and the obvious hole of one missing. I told Linda and John about my electrical issue, and when they dropped me off at my house, John walked around with me to look for the GFCI outlet. I suddenly remembered it, in the garage, in a tiny rectangle cut out of the pegboard that held Charlie's tools, two wrenches hiding it.

July 5, Saturday

I'd been blogging for nine months at First Draft: Laying Down the Words, and today I posted for the first time since Charlie died.

Blog: "Life and Not and Lilies"
Posted: July 5, 2008
The house is quiet now. The kids have gone home—son, daughter-in-law, son, and girlfriend. I couldn't have made it without them the past week.

Besides silence, the house is filled with the sweet, sweet scent of lilies. I must do something about that before it overwhelms me. I thought my husband had a stomach

virus—or maybe salmonella—and went out for saltines and ginger ale. But that wasn't it, and after teams of doctors and surgeons in two hospitals worked to save his life over a thirty-eight-hour period, he died one week ago of an aortic dissection, a catastrophic event.

And so . . . .

The First Month

I sat at the breakfast table, the one Charlie bought in Pittsburgh when he lived there and worked for Alcoa. My elbows rested on the glass top, and my forearms lay out in front of me, palms down, fingers spread. I wore my mama's wedding ring on the right hand. She had given it to me on her fiftieth wedding anniversary. On the left hand, ring finger, I wore three specially designed gold bands: an engagement ring with blue sapphires, a wedding ring melted down from my father's first gold band—my mother had bought him a new one—and a one-year anniversary ring with white sapphires.

But I wasn't married any more.

My arms tingled. It was dusk outside the bay window. The big, old scrub trees, eleven of them that have stood in the same spot for more than a century—pasture-turned-subdivision back yard—changed from green to black as light faded. The hum was taking over my head. The ceiling fan whirled above me. A layer of dust had piled up on the edges of the white blades. My heart pounded in my throat, sending vibrations through my cheeks and down my neck. Air wouldn't go all the way down my windpipe, so I gasped to force it through. The four walls of the room started to close in on me.

I felt the edges. Of my body. Curling up.

I could picture it in my mind as it was happening. Skin. Like old parchment paper. In the Seventies, I decoupaged, and for an aged effect, I'd tear around the page of art or script, then hold a lighted match to the edges for a burned look. That's what this felt like. My edges were charred, cracking, and peeling up, leaving a red, oozing rawness underneath.

I knew what it was. The shock was wearing off. It was lifting off of me to expose a pain like I'd never known.

Crippling grief. Uncontrollable anger. Guilt bearing down. Devastating loneliness. The need to scream—a tribal, uninhibited scream. I made fists and cried.

All these feelings, I didn't know what to do with.

And I couldn't. Get. My breath.

I couldn't bear this. Couldn't go any further. I knew Saturday would never end. And if it did. Sunday. Would come.

Then, it was like a balm spreading over me and soothing my grief-sick soul. I realized I didn't have to live like this.

I looked at the black bookshelf across the room and focused on three shelves that held the books of local Williamson County authors. I knew all these writers—went to their book signings. Sitting on one shelf in front of some books was a china Smokey hound dog statue—the UT mascot—in a pose of running and jumping over a log. Next to it was another china figurine of three blue tick pups playing. The shelf below held a china Santa Claus dressed in an orange suit throwing a Tennessee football. Charlie was a UT football season ticketholder. He shared tickets with customers, and we always went to two or three games every fall at Neyland Stadium in Knoxville. He was the biggest UT fan in the world.

That precious life was gone.

I didn't have to feel this pain. There was a way out. Yes, indeed there was.

Suicide.

What could be worse than where I was?

At the same time, I knew I needed help.

Thoughts of suicide are normal during intense grief. You just have to quickly get your head about you and not let yourself slide down into a pit you cannot get out of.

I grabbed the phone, dug out a number, and called a woman I worked with in a local writers' organization. She'd known loss, too. "I need help," I told her. "I need counseling."

She did the footwork and set me up with a counselor at Brentwood Baptist Church. She knew that in my state, looking up a phone number was more than I could handle. She was the perfect friend in my crisis. She took my request seriously, acted immediately and compassionately, and kept a check on me. All I had to do was show up. I could make it three days till I saw the counselor.

Sunday morning, I turned to the crossword puzzle in _The Tennessean_ newspaper. I thought I would never attempt a crossword puzzle again. I didn't even want to see a grid. That was something Charlie and I did together. He was the one who could sit down and fill out the whole thing without stopping. I couldn't. I could maybe fill in eight or ten words—fifteen on a good day with an easy puzzle. We kept about five puzzles going, leaving them in strategic places around the house. "I corrected all your mistakes," he'd tell me. A few times, only a few, I got to correct his, and those were gold medal moments.

I started filling in answers. I passed my usual few. How was I doing this? I kept going somehow. The grid was filling up with letters and words. I kept writing answers in. In half an hour I filled in the whole thing. For the first time in my life, I'd answered all of a crossword puzzle. I laughed out loud. Then I tossed my pencil across the newsprint. "Humph," I said. I knew what had just happened. Charlie was here in this room with me. He was working the puzzle through me, for me, putting the answers in my head. There was no doubt about it. I couldn't have worked that puzzle by myself. He was showing me that he could still be with me. Communication mind to mind and spirit to spirit could take place through the veil that separated husband and wife after death. It was the only way he could let me know he was still here and that he could put answers in my head. He needed to do that in order to take care of GENISYS.

There are some moments people can't ever take away from you or explain them away. That was one of them. In the coming days, I would feel Charlie comfort me. In moments of deep grief and sobs, I would feel the pain lift and calm come. In agony over business decisions and how to handle them, I would hear him say, "Don't worry, do it this way, and it will work." I would feel him present and answering in the big-picture judgments he always thought I couldn't see. This man would show up even after death to take care of me and his business.

Meanwhile, the business—I couldn't sit on it. I couldn't rack up rent payments due. I had to be out of the office complex before August 1. Sometimes, no matter how you feel, no matter how much sorrow swamps you, you have to take care of business. I learned to separate and divide—to store my anguish and grief behind me while I took care of important issues at hand.

I had three weeks to clean out, throw away, sell furniture and inventory, and move everything that was left out of the office space and into the garage at home. Three weeks. Three weeks wasn't much time to handle the stuff of a man who kept everything he'd ever had all his life. He still had his biology bug collection from high school. He had rock collections from elementary, arrowhead collections, a collection of old radio tubes from when he was a ham operator as a teenager. He kept boxes of old computer parts and different sizes of patch cables, he kept an inventory of basic new parts, he kept used components he could pull out and use permanently or temporarily to keep a customer up and running.

I remembered that after Dad had a heart attack, quintuple bypass surgery, and a month-long hospital stay, Mama fussed about the storage room of the barber shop he owned. "We're cleaning all that junk out. I don't want to have to do it by myself when you die."

My job now was dismantling the office.

I'd once told Charlie that if anything ever happened to him, I'd throw all his junk away. I didn't mean it. But now I was really doing it—rummaging through boxes and drawers, tossing stuff in garbage bags, loading it in the car to drive to the dumpster.

My eyes were so tear-blurred I could barely see. "You died on me!" I cried. "I don't need all this junk."

I pulled my Subaru Outback in front of the office and opened the rear hatch. I loaded it up with boxes of used hard drives, ancient floppy drives, software for DOS, CD-ROM drives, old how-to trade books, dozens of bins of screws and connectors and other nouns that only an engineer would know.

"I'm so sorry I'm throwing your stuff away. I don't need it, I don't have room for it, and what would I ever do with it anyway?" I cried harder than I'd ever cried in my life.

The office complex was big—several streets, several buildings, and many offices. At the back of the complex was a dumpster. I drove to it with my first load of Charlie's stuff. I opened the back hatch, took out the first box, and threw it in. It made a loud noise hitting the metal side, the contents rattling and disbursing and echoing off the bottom steel. I threw another, then another. I threw each successive one harder. I was sobbing and throwing with all the strength I had. I was hurting the boxes and shattering things in those boxes, breaking and scattering stuff to smithereens. If I had to be hurt and broken, then all that other stuff that had belonged to him did, too. "You died on me!" The push and pain of effort felt good. The noise felt good. I kept wiping sweat and tears on the shoulder fabric of my shirt. Tears were falling to the pavement around my feet. I was throwing away pain and anger, and there was an endless supply of both. I didn't care about the spectacle I was making of myself.

It's okay to be angry when you lose something so vital—angry at the person you lost, angry at the world, angry at God, angry toward friends who have not experienced loss, angry that the loss happened, angry at having to go through this painful process.

It was good to physically do something to get the pain and anger out.

A truck pulled up and stopped beside me. Two men were in the front seat—the complex's maintenance crew.

"This dumpster is for the use of the tenants here. Do you have an office in this complex?"

"Yes." I pushed out the answer, still sobbing and not caring. "I just inherited one." The heat was bearing down on me, and I could see the sun shining off the hair at the sides of my face, my hair rumpled and curling in the humidity. "My husband had a business somewhere up front—I don't even remember the number right now. The name of it is GENISYS. You can go up there and look for yourself if you want to. He died." I was still shaking and crying. "I'm cleaning out the office and throwing his junk away."

"Yes, ma'am. Okay. That's fine. Let us know if you need any help." They drove away.

For days, I boxed, loaded, and hauled. I cried during the whole process—every day, every trip to the dumpster. I cried out loud. I held the boxes or big parts or old furniture over my head, heaving them as hard as I could, making them bang against the metal dumpster sides, making them break.

Then I remembered—I'd just had a hysterectomy two and a half months ago. Should I be lifting and hauling all this heavy stuff? I called my gynecologist. Yes, I could lift and throw anything I wanted to.

I had so much adrenaline in my body I could pick up and carry the biggest of objects. And with each crash into the dumpster, I was getting one more piece of anger out.

Occasionally, over the next three weeks, as I dumped the stuff of GENISYS, I would see those two maintenance men. They would pull up to a stop sign a block or two away within the complex and watch me for a minute, then move on. They didn't dare come near me.

During those three weeks, I not only hauled to the dumpster, but I packed things to take home and put prices on stuff to sell. And I cleaned out the garage at home, making room. Mixed in with that, I wrote a business merger contract, had two job interviews, and went to a grief counseling session.

At the counseling session, I told the minister, "I just want to make sure I'm doing this right."

Grieving. Is there a right way?

"Are you always concerned about doing things right?" he asked.

I guessed I was. He told me practical things, like what was happening to my body physically with grief—a continuous flood of stress hormones was being released into my system, producing anxiety. Sleeping rhythms, digestion, metabolism, circulation, and respiration had changed. He showed me how to breathe in order to manage the physical symptoms—breathe in deeply, concentrate, feel it down in my feet. He told me to write a letter to Charlie and say what I needed and wanted to say, make apologies, and tie up loose ends, then to disburse the letter with Charlie's ashes when I felt the time was right.

All those drives up Franklin Road to the office, I kept noticing the sign in front of a church—big, black letters stuck on a white marquis: "You think this is hot? Try hell." Hell didn't scare me any more. I'd been living in it for four weeks now.

July 25, the appointed moving day, came, and the sons were home again for a few days. We rented a U-Haul. I'd sold a lot of office furniture on Craigslist and gotten the word out to other tenants in the complex. Other business owners were coming by and buying things, like chairs, end tables, desks, pictures, and shelves. One man had his eye on the two Werner ladders, an eight-foot and a six-foot.

"I'll take those," he said, "and that battery backup. For a hundred dollars." He pointed to a black backup.

"I can't sell them for that amount."

"What are you going to do with 'em? You don't need 'em. I'll take 'em off your hands."

"No, I don't think so."

"You'll just have to store 'em." He kept pushing.

Todd and Cory saw what was happening and instantly stepped to my sides, and I could see in my peripheral vision their chins jutting out, their feet planted, and their chests puffed out.

"You heard her," Todd said. "Either offer a reasonable price or move on out."

There could have been a fight, I thought.

"Don't give Charlie's stuff away," they told me. "Let us handle people if they're unfair."

I felt protected.

Human nature makes even good folks try to take advantage of a vulnerable woman.

There was a tremendous amount of stuff left in the office of GENISYS Systems Group. We packed up workbenches and stools, shelves, desks, kitchen furniture and supplies, ladders, inventory, books and software, customer job files and billing files, hundreds of patch cables and RAM—new and used—and old monitors and computers that I couldn't dispose of because of sensitive data on the hard drives. There were two GENISYS systems in the office— old ones that had recently been taken out of service at customer locations—from when our company built computers, back in the day before Micron, Gateway, and Dell took the market and made it so that small companies like GENISYS couldn't compete price- wise. I wanted to keep those.

As the truck got full and the office got empty and the day wound down, the tears started to roll and wouldn't stop. I stood in that dark, empty, silent office and knew it was really all over. He was gone. His work was done. I took the GENISYS sign down. I put my finger on the light switch and looked around at the bareness that was once our life. Then I turned out the light.

I cried all the way home.

At home, before filling up the garage with office furniture and supplies, Todd and Cory set up the table saw and took on a construction project—installing a doggy door. I knew I'd eventually have to go to work full-time and leave my dog all day, every day. I needed her to have access to the back yard. Charlie and I had talked about putting in a door, but as an engineer, he had to measure and plan and figure out a way to make it perfect. There was always some aspect he couldn't work out to his satisfaction with the full-length glass-window door we had. I knew the sons with their approach to life would just do it without thinking that it couldn't be done.

I bought a new wooden door with a glass window in the top half to replace the old door with full-length glass panes, and I got a doggy door with a flap and a metal panel that could slip in and lock. The boys measured and sawed and put in the doggy door and then put up the wooden door. It was the first time they ever did a construction project together, and their personalities clashed. Grown men, but they tattled on one another.

"Todd cut too much off the door bottom," Cory told me. "I've got to go out there and fix what he did wrong."

Todd came in huffing. "Cory is so anal. He can just finish it all by himself."

In spite of their differences, they got the job done. I caulked and painted and hung blinds over the top window, and it was a pretty and practical solution.

Now, it was my job to get Chaeli to use it. I wasn't sure I could teach a nine-year-old dog new tricks, but I got down on the floor and pushed my head through the flap. I repeated what would be her new mantra—push it, go outside, tee tee. She didn't mind the coming-in part, but was hesitant about going out at first. My friend Susie came by for a visit and said she'd show her how. She gave the dog a gentle shove from behind. And by golly, that did it. The old pup learned. From then on, she'd push the flap open with her head, hop out the door, walk across the porch decking and down three steps, eat some dead locust shells, sniff the ivy, check the perimeters of her yard, and tee tee. That little blond spaniel was pushing forward in the new, and it brought me some smiles.

There were other things that took me down.

Filing away papers in the home office, I saw them—six manila file folders where there should have been twelve. Every year, the last two days of December at GENISYS, Charlie and I took inventory, and I made up the next year's expense folders: January 2008,

February 2008, March 2008 . . . they should have gone through December 2008, but I was in a hurry last December, and I only did half a year . . . June 2008, and he died at the end of June, and it was all my fault. I made it happen, this death event, his end to life, my having to start over anew. If I'd done the whole year of folders, he might still be alive.

July 31 came, and I signed the merger for the business. For three years I would receive a percentage of the income GENISYS customers generated, so I'd have a small monthly amount coming in to help with expenses. An established Nashville company with a progressive and compassionate owner took over my customers. I could put Charlie's cell phone away and rest in the knowledge that our customers had technicians to call.

GENISYS was gone.

I made it through the first month.

An Open Letter

Blog: "An Open Letter"
Posted: August 3, 2008

My dear husband,

I need to clear the air. I have regrets, guilt, and I need to talk to you about it. I went to a grief counselor and it was recommended that I write you a letter and say what I want to say and then perhaps burn the letter and take the ashes with yours to the Tennessee River beside Neyland Stadium and send them off with you. But I'm keeping you here with me until I resolve my guilt and I'm ready to release you. And I'm saying this openly because I suspect there is a community of us who are caught up in living and don't grasp that we are walking a tightrope between life and death, and then when death comes suddenly, it catches us wishing we'd done it all differently, and it heaps loads of guilt on our backs. What we do with our guilt affects how we grieve and heal. I suspect I will always hold myself somewhat accountable. You were mine to take care of, and I didn't do a good job. We both knew you were the caregiver in our relationship, but that doesn't excuse my actions on that fateful day.

First of all, I'm so sorry I didn't follow my gut feelings. A couple of weeks before you died, I remember looking at you one evening as you sat in your chair watching "Larry King Live" or one of those Lifetime movies you hated, and what I saw made me gush aloud with no tact because it was so vividly blatant.

"My gosh, your face is gray and chalky. What's wrong with you?" You were not happy with my observation. "Nothing," you said, taken aback, "I'm fine." But on subsequent nights, I stole glances at you and you had that same grayish and whitish look and not the pinkish red face I was used to seeing. Maybe this was a sign of the catastrophic event that ultimately took your life. Maybe not. Maybe I should have insisted you go to the doctor. Maybe you'd be alive today if I had. We're talking about your life here, and I didn't do enough to save it. I'm so sorry.

A week before you died, you looked at me one evening and rubbed your legs together and said, "My legs are tingling." I knew with those words that something was wrong with you. Maybe then I should have insisted that you go to the doctor. Maybe you'd be alive today if I had. I'm so sorry. But I know as well as I know my own name that the doctor wouldn't have suspected aortic dissection. After all, many people have tingling legs. My father did all his adult life. He rubbed his legs together like a cricket and complained every night. He lived to be eighty-four and didn't die like you did.

I remember you telling me that your back hurt. "Low back?" I asked. "No," you said, "between my shoulder blades." Your olive green eyes looked into mine, wanting an answer. You'd never hurt there. Now I suspect it was caused by the aneurysm or tear, or the process of aortic dissection beginning. I couldn't have known, but I wish I'd done something to stop that horrific process. After all, it was your life. I'm so sorry.

I always teased and told you I knew everything and I could diagnose your aches and pains, but when it really mattered, I didn't know anything, and I couldn't diagnose you, and I couldn't take care of you, and I didn't, and I'm so sorry. I've spent my entire life trying to make things all right, and I couldn't make this all right.

I keep thinking back to that Friday morning, a little over a month ago. You woke up at three, sick. You didn't wake me then, but told me at five, when I got up. You just told me you had diarrhea. I thought you had a stomach virus, or maybe salmonella from the tomatoes we had eaten. You thought so, too. I was a little miffed with you because in your job you were always touching people's mice and keyboards and catching things, even though you used hand sanitizer religiously. I even tried to stay away from you because in two days, I was leaving for Asheville to be with Cory while he had an endoscopy for a persistent problem, a feeling like something was in his throat. I couldn't go to this procedure if I caught a stomach virus. I sprayed the house with Lysol and regret this display of drama. I'm so sorry I didn't put my arms around you and my face against yours and hold you and ask what I could do to help. Instead, I worked with a vengeance that morning. I paid bills, I did invoices for GENISYS, I went to the bank, I went to Publix to get you crackers and ginger ale—dear God, you could have died while I was gone!—I tried to complete all my work so I could be away a few days. I didn't know how serious it was, I didn't know how incredibly sick you were, and I'm so sorry.

You didn't tell me there was blood with the diarrhea, and lots of it, until later in the morning. I called the doctor, but by then the staff was at lunch. "Let's just be there at 1:30 when they get back," I said. "Or do you think this is an emergency and we should go on to the hospital?" You said it would be 1:30 before you could get your clothes on anyway. As we drove up under the canopy, you said you'd need a wheel chair. I still didn't understand how sick you were. I got a nurse, and we wheeled you in.

I knew it was something bad when you told the doctor that it felt like someone had jabbed a broom handle down your throat. You hadn't told me that, and I keep seeing the image of you illustrating that to the doctor. He wrote up orders to admit you to the hospital, and I wheeled you back out to the car.

"Okay, get up and get in the car," I said. You didn't move. I didn't realize you couldn't move. "C'mon," I said, patting you, then trying to hold your arm and help you. You looked around at me with twitchy movements, and I'm not sure if you were passing out or seizing or what, but I remember shaking your shoulder and yelling, "Stay with me, Charlie!" I ran inside for help. A doctor and nurse came running outside. I told her to call 9-1-1, which she did. A team took you inside and put you on a table and held your legs up and I helped them and they started an IV and tried to stabilize you. The ambulance arrived and took you away, and I was scared out of my mind, but I still didn't know how sick you were, and I'm so sorry.

I hurried to the ER.

They kept your IV going, they started giving you blood, you screamed with pain and writhed and pulled out all your tubes, and they couldn't give you anything for pain because your BP was so low they couldn't even get a reading except by Doppler. You said, "It's bad, isn't it?" and I should have said yes, but all I did was try and calm you. I thought they could correct your problem with surgery, I thought you'd be okay.

You wouldn't have wanted the five hours of surgery, the life flight to Vanderbilt, six more hours of surgery, then an additional hour of surgery, during which you succumbed. You always said you wanted to "go" quickly. You lived thirty-eight hours. It was a violently invasive thirty-eight hours, and I can't get over the catastrophic nature of it and never will. I'm so sorry you had to go through all that.

Most of all, I'm so sorry I took you to the doctor and you never got to come home again. Your life was full of loose ends. You never got to tell the dog goodbye. You had jobs for customers pending, inventory ordered. You had season tickets for UT football, hotel reservations made. You bought parts to fix the grill, you were going to fix the headlight on my car, you were going to clean the gutters out, and you wanted to buy a bicycle like mine, or a motorbike. It's like we were walking along having a normal life like everybody else and all of a sudden we were at the edge of a cliff, and this was truly where the world ended. Only it was you that fell off, and not me, and I'm so sorry it ended for you and it ended this way. And I want you to know it ended for me, too, in a different way.

Our wedding vows that we composed together concluded with "I want to endure all things with you. I want to walk home to God with you." You kept your promise to me. I cannot keep mine to you, and I'm so sorry.

In baring my innermost soul to the whole world, I am in hopes that others will remember my experience and ponder and prevent the likes from happening to them, the guilt and regrets part, that is. I am letting you know that I feel so unworthy to have had you, so undeserving of your goodness and generous spirit, so unworthy as a person. I am so sorry I didn't do better with what I had.

Yours,
Kathy

Emotional and Sensitive

How would I get through this? How does someone who is emotional and sensitive get over the death of her husband?

My mother gave me this three-word tag—"emotional and sensitive." All my life she told me that's what I was. Even before puberty, when I had no hormones to trigger a response that could be considered such. She said it as though it was my downfall, a flaw in my character, something we'd always have to watch out for and work around.

"Be careful what you say around Kathy," she'd tell my sister. "She's emotional and sensitive. You have to take care of her."

My little sister was the strong one. I was the weak one. That's the way it always was.

I grew to expect being described that way, to believe it myself. It was pounded into my head. As I lived through my teen years, I played it all out. I got my feelings hurt, I had disappointments, I had hormones, and I cried, and I figured it was because I was emotional and sensitive. My mama even told my husband, she told my children—and any time I displayed any emotion over anything, valid or maybe not so much, she repeated her longtime stance. "Kathy is emotional and sensitive."

I hated to be tagged this way. The whole image of a girl, then a woman, with her head down, tight-timid positioning of her lips, and shoulders curled, someone people had to walk on eggshells around, infuriated me. And when confronted with my tag description, I would fly off the handle, confirming I really was emotional and sensitive. I didn't want to be that person.

There was nothing I could do to shake the image. Everybody's going to cry at one time or another, and everybody is going to get their feelings hurt. Why was it so bad when I reacted after legitimately being wronged?

Emotional and sensitive. Compound predicate adjectives. The adjectives were always used together. Never separately.

They defined me—like a label stuck smack to my forehead.

The honest truth was that I never saw myself this way. I always saw myself as standing strong, as taking a lick and getting back up and forging on. Sure, I got upset and cried. But so did other people. My sister did. My friends did. Why was I singled out?

When my first husband divorced me, life's hurts had piled up so high that I put a stop to it all. I stopped feeling. I stopped crying. I didn't cry for fifteen years. I closed my heart and grew rock hard. I wouldn't let anything shake that solid image. It took three weeks before I could drop one tear when my father died.

What was I going to do now? My husband was dead. I needed to cry. I did cry every day. I came to accept the part of me that felt emotion.

Then one day I got out my baby book to do some research for a personal essay I was writing. The book was pink satin and had a bouquet of flowers on the front, along with scalloped brown age stains. I opened it, turned the pages, and looked at black-and-white pictures—me with my first puppy, Timbo; me in a metal stroller, crying, my mouth an upside-down U; my daddy holding me, his foot propped up on the bumper of a nineteen-forties-something Plymouth.

There, on page fourteen, what was this? A HOROSCOPE wheel? It was a circle of light blue wedges, each one with the name of a month, its astrological sign, and a description of the person born under that sign. The months were separated by long, pink ribbons, held by naked, blond cherubs, appearing to walk and turn the wheel like it was a Maypole. My mama had circled my birth month of September with a brown crayon. I read about myself.

SEPTEMBER—VIRGO (Virgin)—Keen. Alert mind. Introspective. Emotional and sensitive.

Well. Now I knew. I'd lived my whole life under this umbrella for no more reason than there it was, written in my baby book, under my horoscope, so it had to be true. Mama had read it and believed it. And scooped me up and put all the pieces of me in that category and held me to it all my life. Why couldn't she have described me as keen and with an alert mind?

Yet about six decades later, here I was, emotional and sensitive. Only now, I had a good reason to be.

The First Year

Peeple were all the time asking how I was. "Fine," I'd always say. Then I learned FINE was an acronym for Fouled up, Insecure, Neurotic, Emotional wreck.

That was a fine assessment of the first year because the first year was all about a slow separation from a life that used to be. The first year: letting go, holding on, moving on.

In all those tugs and releases, I intuitively made myself feel the loss and shoulder through the grief. And all the way, I fought to keep up my writing and editing and blogging, hanging on to the only part of my identity that remained. I devoted time each day to walking hard and fast and commanding the hurt to get out of my body. "Go away! You cannot have me!" I'd shake my hands as I walked, throwing the pain out of my fingertips to the sidewalk.

I settled in to the lonely quiet. I took on the Death Duties— tying up loose ends and taking care of belongings in a way that would please and honor Charlie. I did what felt right at the moment.

During the first month, I raked all Charlie's socks and underwear out of his chest-of-drawers and threw them away. I figured nobody would want those. I offered jeans, shirts, and jackets to the men of the family. He had new Diamond Gusset jeans, one hundred percent American-made. He always had his shirts laundered at the cleaners, and they were all Lands End with little engineer-like grids or tight stripes, or shirts with University of Tennessee orange in them or UT logos. There was one batch of shirts at the cleaners when he died, and I left it there for six months, because I couldn't bear doing something as routine as picking up clothes at the laundry, and I couldn't bear seeing his shirts hanging there wrapped in plastic. He had a collection of barn jackets, orange leather jackets, and black leather jackets.

I held on to the black leather Titans jacket. He had worn it every day during his last few winters.

I also kept the long leather coat from his Pittsburgh days, his slippers, robes, and work boots.

I put all his shoes in the Outback and drove up Hillsboro Road to the Goodwill store. The warehouse seemed dark—scant lights way up high. It was a gray place with piles of bulging black bags and tinges of color scattered about—old Fisher Price reds and blues, yellow plastic flowers, and the silvers of small appliances. It smelled like feet, the gym at my kids' old school, and dust. I opened my sack of loafers, tie-ups, sneakers, sandals, and deck shoes, and the receiving employee in a loose beige shirt threw them—clunk!—pair by pair—clunk!—all the way across the big room in a heap with others, all old, battered, and worn. Clunk! Like in a mass grave. I thought it was a harsh thing to do, but the man didn't know those shoes had belonged to Charlie. I wanted to tell him to please be careful, that those were my husband's, and he just died. But I only stood there, sucked in a breath, held it, mouth open, and didn't say anything. The room whirled around me. An urge came to go get them, pick them up gently, and take them back home with me.

"Do you want a receipt?" the man said.

"Yes." How cold was it to get a receipt for my deceased husband's shoes and deduct them from my income taxes as a donation?

With each belonging I gave away, another piece of Charlie was gone, and I'd cry all over again.

But I held on to Charlie's last voice mail: "Well, I guess you're trying to reach me while I'm trying to reach you. I guess we'll find each other soon."

I boxed up the old dishes, the black square set he brought to the marriage, and stored them in the garage, because I couldn't bring myself to drop them in the garbage can. I needed something new. The old was too much a reminder of him, and that was an easy "familiar" to change. I picked out a colorful Sedona hand-painted set.

I threw out the old bedspread, a green and burgundy one we'd bought in Atlanta twelve years earlier. I bought new sheets, new pillow shams, a new bedspread—another easy "familiar" to change—and I got what I liked. I'd always had to consider a man's preferences—no flowers, no pinks or purples, no lace. Yet I chose a masculine brown with accents of baby blue.

August came, and down in Mississippi, eight fertilized eggs sat in a petri dish. Eight eggs became five. These five would be watched, and the two healthiest would be selected for implantation. One might be Winston Hardy, Charlie's penname and my maiden name. I might become a grandmother. I wanted to tell Charlie about it.

I wanted to talk to someone. I needed to share my feelings of loss and have the support of others who understood, so I joined a grief recovery support group at Christ Presbyterian Church in Nashville. In this group were three other women—one had lost a close friend, one her mother, and one her grandmother. All three were single.

The class included a video of people expressing their grief over losses and a workbook with questions for me to answer about my own experience and a journal section for me to write down my feelings, all designed to help me learn how to live with grief and how to begin to heal.

I had to pinpoint how I felt. _How would I describe the pain?_ "A tingling that rolls down from the backs of my arms, leaving me weak all over and sucking the breath out of me. A hairball of anguish and agony in my throat that never goes away. Legs that don't want to move forward," I wrote.

I'd often think back to the days when I was a girl, or even a young woman, with a light step, a skip, sunshine all around me, and I was innocent, carefree, playful, happy, vibrant, running barefoot in the Bermuda grass in my back yard or down a pine-needle path in the woods on Papaw's farm. Oh, how I wanted to go back to that time!

But now "my bones are in agony. My soul is in anguish. How long, O LORD, how long?" (Psalm 6:23 KJV)

What concerns did I have as I walked through the healing process? "The rest of my life will be spent as a weakened structure with the threads of his fabric removed, with the reality that I am not a whole person. I want to be whole, but I can't."

I had to deal with my spiritual struggle. *Was God dwelling in me?* "He's in there—DEEP," I wrote. "I felt He left me, so I pulled away, too. I have let the vines cover Him up."

The loss of my husband brought layers of losses that I had to recognize and mourn. I was slowly gaining understanding of all the big things, as well as the little things, now gone—husband, best friend, companion, confidant, around-the-house helper. GENISYS. Job. Income. Dreams. Eventually, my house.

And shrimp. No more shrimp on the grill. He loved to cook on his Weber. Not only shrimp, but thick steaks injected with marinade and garlic cloves and ribs made with his own special recipe of pickling spices and barbecue sauce. I couldn't bear the loss of grilled dinners.

No more salt and pepper. He was the one who took care of details, like filling up the salt and pepper mills. He'd buy sea salt crystals and red and black peppercorns and make sure the mills never got low.

No more batteries for clocks. The black marble mantel clock and the two wall clocks would now just exist, their hands stilled. He took care of keeping them running.

The one who saw to the things that ran down, went out, or broke was not here anymore.

I'd never had to change light bulbs, but since Electrical Engineer Charlie died, bulbs in electrical fixtures started going out everywhere. I'd had to change the one in the glass globe over the glass-top breakfast table twice in a matter of weeks. The light on the back porch went out every week, it seemed. I finally just gave up. It could stay dark out there forever for all I cared. Then the front porch light went out. What was up with all that? I knew it was Charlie making them go out, and I anguished and screamed at him. "Stop it! I'm sorry I let you die, I'm sorry for everything, I can't handle all this, so just stop it!" No more lights went out.

Then the vacuum cleaner broke. It was stopped up somewhere in the long pipe that looped around between the floor surface and the dirt-filled canister. I carried it outside in the garage, took the pipe off, and cried because I shouldn't have to be fixing appliances. I was never one given to cursing, especially out loud, but bad words started spewing out of my mouth under the tears, and I was stringing them together, all five bad words I had picked up in my lifetime.

I slammed the vacuum cleaner down on the hard concrete— once, twice.

Then I went to the workbench and found a long hanger-like wire with a hook on it dangling from the pegboard. Charlie must have used it to do this same job. I sat on the concrete floor and stuck the wire in that pipe and picked and pulled out globs of dust and dog hair all matted together. But the tight clump was too deep. I couldn't get to it, so I stretched the pipe out of the garage into the driveway, like a long black snake. I plugged in the leaf blower, put the end of the blower against the opening of the vacuum pipe, and turned it on full blast. The force of the wind blew that clog out and whooshed it down the driveway.

"Don't mess with me," I growled, following it, blowing it into the street.

Changing the HVAC filters shouldn't have been a monumental job. I'd always changed the downstairs filter. But there was a return on the ceiling at the top of the stairs for the second unit, and that was a terrifying job for me. I had to get a step-stool and set it an inch from the edge of the landing at the top of the stairs. I was scared of heights, and climbing up the stool's three steps at the top of the fifteen stairs was enough to set me off. Charlie had always changed that filter.

At one session of my grief group, I told the three other women how light bulbs were going out, things were breaking, and changing a high-on-the-ceiling filter was something I could barely handle. I reached for a Kleenex and wiped the blur from my eyes. Nobody was saying anything to comfort me. I looked at them, and they were sitting there staring at me, with their mouths wide open, like *So?* Then it hit me.

"Oh. Y'all are all single. You have to do this stuff all the time. Well." I smiled and felt silly and shallow with my complaints.

In this new normal semblance of a life, I had to fix things that broke, keep up the maintenance on the house, and get the oil changed in two cars. If I didn't know how to do something, I had to figure it out. If I bought something, like a fire pit from Home Depot, I had to follow directions and put it together. I had to be . . . a man.

I also had to be the breadwinner.

Seven weeks after Charlie died and three weeks after I merged the business, I started a new job. I'd used a search agency in Brentwood, and they came through with a position in an advertising agency just a few weeks before the 2008 economic collapse and the clamp-down of the job market. If I hadn't gotten a job right then, I probably wouldn't have gotten one. This job was an eight-to-five, a paycheck, survival, a blessing, and I was grateful for it.

Still in the high hum of grief, I carried out my duties on the job as best as I could. On the commute to and from, I drove the quiet backroads—up Hillsboro Road, through a Grassland neighborhood, over country-road twists and turns, under canopies of scrub trees and vines, past peacocks and horses and big houses on a hill, then up Granny White Pike. Lunches, I'd drive to a little church of Christ near my office, park under an old oak tree, and eat a sandwich. At the appointed evening leave time, I'd rush to my car, snap the seat belt, and pull out of the parking lot, anxious to get home and make sure my dog was all right.

All the way, I'd cry hard and out loud. There was something about being in the car. It was tight and closed in, and my attention was narrowed in to me and my loss. For the twenty-five-minute drive, I had nothing to do but think and mourn. I was so lonely, missed my husband and my old life, and felt my new life would be this way forevermore. Once I got home I had four walls closing in and more crying to do. Life consisted of a menial job to pay the bills, tears, four walls to sit inside, the quiet lonely, and that was all.

My dog gave me the only reason to exist. She needed me. And I needed her.

Evenings after work, I'd put together a quick dinner, then call my mother. We'd have a conversation while I ate. Mama didn't have anyone to talk to either or any activities out of the house, except church once a week. She needed me. And I needed her. My talks with my mother were the only human conversations, not work related, that I'd have for days and sometimes weeks on end, except for weekly grief group sessions, monthly writers group meetings, and brief daily checks from my sons.

After I talked to Mama, I'd get on Facebook. I didn't have family around me inside my four walls, and it was soothing to have this community of people at my fingertips. I could keep up with them, communicate with them, make comments on what they were doing, and feel the motion and emotion of the activities they were involved in. I felt people around me. Facebook became my family.

One evening I'd just gotten home from work, and I was scrambling to fix the dog and me some supper, so I could call Mom before seven, her bedtime, when the phone rang.

"Are you responsible for the estate of Charles Rhodes?"

"What business is it of yours?"

"I need to know if you are the responsible party."

It was the Death Department of a major credit card company of the Visa Charlie used for business expenses.

"Why do you need to know?"

"When are you going to pay this bill?"

Rage bled over me so red that I trembled. "Do you see a month when that bill wasn't paid?"

"No."

"Do you notice that more than the minimum payment has been made each month?"

"Yes."

"Who do you think is paying that?"

"I just want to know when it's all going to be paid."

"I'll pay off that balance when I am good and ready to. Don't you ever call me again." Click, ding. I'd planned to clear the balance in the coming month, but after this intimidating call, I wasn't about to. The service charge was worth accumulating just so it wouldn't look like I was scared into paying.

My biggest challenge came from the telephone company. They sent GENISYS a bill for breach of contract in the amount of $394.38, because Charlie died and could no longer keep his phone service at the office he no longer had because I merged the business and moved out and officially shut it down.

GENISYS was probably the last business in the country to give up our ISDN line, simply because we did not want to enter a contract with the phone company. We called on at least three occasions to add high-speed Internet and change our service plan, but backed away every time because we were afraid of a long-term contract. Then when we finally negotiated an agreement, we made sure to ask for short-term. I signed that twenty-four-month contract thirty months before this incident. Somehow the word "renewable" had slipped into the fine print. When you signed up with the phone company for a twenty-four-month term, it automatically renewed for another twenty-four months every time it expired. In other words, it appeared the contract was eternal, even if you weren't, unless you took action and wrote the phone company a letter one hundred eighty days before you died to tell them you didn't want the contract to renew. I had a one-day warning that my husband was going to die.

The phone company said they were sorry their customer died, but he still had to pay the penalty for canceling his service early. They couldn't help it, couldn't do a thing about it. A contract is a legal and binding document, after all, and even though Charlie was dead and his company didn't exist, he had to pay that contract termination fee. They had no provision for extenuating circumstances like death. It was just too bad. "Make payment arrangements," the representative said.

I eventually had to go through the Tennessee Regulatory Authority to get the cancellation fee removed.

I directed my grief-anger at big companies that were harsh and unreasonable. I cried from the gut during the process because the tactics and procedures were unjust, because it was making an animal out of me, because it was an abuse of my husband's good name and business practices. I had to protect my husband.

August 25, on what would've been the sixty-fourth wedding anniversary of my mama and dad, if he hadn't died, two fertilized eggs were implanted in my daughter-in-law's womb. There were two blastocytes. Or embryos, or babies. If they both "took," my son was going to make me a grandmother of twins.

August 28, the two-month anniversary of Charlie's death, I had to write down my feelings about my journey of mourning for my grief group.

"I wake up and it is right there as though it never left. Like a dark cloud, it hovers, settling down on me, like a low ceiling that I must duck and walk under the rest of the day. It is claustrophobic, it is gripping, it weakens me."

Grief. Where there used to be fulfilling joy and a light step and happiness and lots of laughter and playfulness and that feeling that I was never alone, that I had a soul mate who loved me and supported me and lifted me to the heights of a bright world, now there was grief. Grief was my companion.

Grief pressed down. Then I'd break through and function. I might have smiled. I might have even laughed at something the dog did or when a friend drank a Margarita and confessed things about her first marriage. Then I'd remember. Oh yes, grief. My body would go limp, my back curl, and I'd succumb to that feeling of loss and sadness and fall into it physically, emotionally, and spiritually. It would come on suddenly, it would come on hard, and it would take me over.

All my life I'd heard people say that the first year after a death was hard because of the DREADED FIRSTS—the first birthday, anniversary, and the holidays without that loved one. It was like those dates were bolded and shadowed to stand out on the calendar page. I saw them coming, and I dreaded it, I built up emotions, I knew it was going to be bad, I anticipated how horrible it was going to be, and I suffered even before the day arrived. Then the day came and ended—without much fanfare.

Moving on meant living through these dates.

My blog, set up originally to be about writing, went to grief that first year. My posts captured the zig of the raw feelings of all those Dreaded Firsts. They also showed the zag of sweet things.

My birthday came first—September 4. A year older, but still in my fifties—way too young to be one of those wid— . . . wid— . . . W-persons. (I hated that word!) My friends—Susie, Colleen, and Currie—took me out to Boxwood Bistro, an upscale affair at The Factory of Franklin that had white tablecloths, shrimp and grits, and popcorn ice cream.

I didn't get any blue sapphires this year, though, or pink ones, and Charlie didn't get to go to Jared's to get me any birthstone jewelry.

But I did get something blue and pink for my birthday.

Blog: "It's official."
Posted: September 4, 2008
That was the subject of an email I got today from Todd: "It's official." I knew what it meant before I read the body of the email, and a smile started spreading out almost to my ears.

WE'RE PREGNANT!

Pregnant. Having a baby. Maybe two babies.

Life goes on. There won't be a Poppy. Charlie had already been tagged with that name when the process of in vitro was first discussed.

This is a lovely surprise on today of all days—my birthday!

Because it was LIFE and life is always filled with big moons and tidal waves, gentle streams and sunshine, and variety, things came along that gave reason for rejoicing. The first year was full of both mourning and joy. Like a sunrise on a cloudy day, there was a glowing line of light and yellow and magenta that cast ripples of pink on top of gray.

Blog: "Twins!"

Posted: September 22, 2008

Twins. Two healthy babies. Two strong heartbeats.

Due late April.

Did I say twins?

The cycle of life, the cycle of seasons—it was autumn, and winter soon, with wind and ice, and after winter, spring would come and bring babies and joy, but before spring, more months of cold and mourning.

Blog: "Three Months"

Posted: September 27, 2008

The calendar on the ledge above the coffee pot still says June 27. He tore off the previous day's page when he got his first cup of coffee that morning. He was dying then, but he didn't know it. June 27 was the last day he poured coffee in our kitchen and the last day he spent with me in the home we built together.

He had a head full of thick, black, curly hair. He shouldn't have died.

Right now, I would give anything in this world to have one of his hugs. He was the best hugger in the world. I could sink into him and stay there, and the world would melt away. I fell in love with him after just one hug. That, and his voice. It was deep and strong, yet soothing. I fell asleep many times listening to him talk.

It is a new world. I'm not happy in it yet—HAPPY is not in my vocabulary any more. It just doesn't apply to life now. I mean, what is there to be happy about? But I'm settling into the newness. It has been three months. I play and laugh with the dog, I work, I walk, I ride my bike, I mow the yard, I hang out with friends, I go to meetings and events, I write and edit, I drink a little wine, and I'm getting used to the loneliness, the aloneness, the quiet, the void.

I'm fine. *FINE.*

Four days ago on my six-in-the-morning walk, I looked up at the sky for the first time in three months. I've been looking down, struggling to make my legs move, focusing on getting the right foot forward, then the left. I know more about what aggregate looks like than the workers who poured and smoothed it. I had forgotten what the lightening Prussian blue sky looked like. It was crisp, the air was cool, and there was a pearl sliver of moon low in the sky. It felt good to look up. It was somehow a turning point.

Blog: "Four Months"
Posted: October 29, 2008

Yes, it was four months. Yesterday. And I would not let myself go there. But today I will.

I will not bury it. I've buried too much.

I'm talking about my grief.

Anyone who has read my blog consistently in the last four months since my husband died has witnessed the ups and downs—the depths of guilt and despair, the joys of new life in the twelve-week-old twin fetuses that are my grandchildren, and the normal, everyday things of life, including the writer within who is trying to pen a memoir, as well as a novel. That's the way my life is. I'm going to write it as I feel it because I have a need to get it out. I don't want it bottled up or stuffed down. I don't think that's healthy. I went to my doctor a few weeks ago and asked him what I should do to combat the harmful hormones that grief causes and how I can stop the damage they are doing to my body. "Exercise," he said. So early mornings I walk, and I walk hard and with purpose and with command, and I lecture the evils that are trying to fill and consume me. "Go away, I will fight you, you cannot have me, you will not bring me down."

In grief group we talked about writing a Grief Letter to our friends because they didn't understand what it was like to lose a significant somebody, and so I did:

Dear friends,

I never thought I would be at this point in my life in my fifties.

I remember I never knew what to say to other women who had lost a spouse. Should I just be quiet and back away and give her time to heal and then I will come around and be her friend again when she's okay? Now I see it in a few of you. You don't know what to say either. And that's okay. It doesn't mean you have to stop being my friend, though. Unless seeing me is a too-painful reminder of what could happen to you.

You will be here one day, too. And then you will know how it feels when a "friend" is too busy with her full and happy life to take a moment to say "hi" to you, after you have just lost your full and happy life. You will know what it is like to come home to a dark and quiet house and to an oven with no warm smells coming from it and to a dog who doesn't yip and yap with glee any more. You will learn what it is like to

eat dinner alone every night. You will know what it is like to
be afraid to open each piece of mail because it might be yet
another company closing this account or sending you to the
estate settlement department and you know you will have to
call and cuss them out and get upset all over again. You will
know what it is like to live with a pounding heart in dread and
fear of the next bad thing that is going to happen, and by golly,
you know it *is* going to happen. You will know what it is like
to be ambushed by a memory, a song, a place.

And you know, because you have been to a grief group,
that all this is normal.

And you know that you will let some friends go, because
they are no longer comfortable with you.

And there are some you will gravitate to.

I thank the Lord above that I am surrounded by many
strong and powerful people. Many of you have been through
much worse than I and pass on your might and determination
and encouragement to me. What would the world be without
folks like you? I am blessed to know you. You are real and deep
and made of substance I want for my own. You are open, you
share, you talk, you ask, you live fully. I want to be like you, I
want to see my struggle through to the top, I want desperately
to be whole again.

And so I fight. Right now, for me.

Sincerely,
Your friend Kathy

The first holiday came. Thanksgiving—the second of the
Dreaded Firsts and the first of five Dreaded Firsts in a five-week
period—Thanksgiving, Charlie's birthday, Chaeli's birthday,
Christmas, our anniversary. Wham slam wham bam wham.

The custom was that Charlie and I always entertained on
Thanksgiving. In the Rhodes family, Charlie had the turkey, and
David had the country ham Christmas breakfast. We might've had

ten to a dozen show up at our house any given November, but not this year. Thanksgiving came in a different way and brought change to the family dynamic.

Blog: "It's a Girl! And a Boy!"
Posted: November 26, 2008

We just finished an ultrasound on this the day before Thanksgiving. I say "we" because I got to be there via conference call and witness the event with my son and daughter-in-law.

Baby A is a girl . . . no doubt about it. Baby B is a boy. "Unmistakable" came the comment from the one holding the wand. Baby B was kicking Baby A, and she was swatting him back.

So now we can buy pink . . . I already have . . . last April, I bought a precious pink outfit, when in vitro was first discussed. And now I can pull out those tiny blue and white oxfords that belonged to my baby boy.

We can call them by name. Winston Hardy. Jillian Dawson. I have a little blue suit my mother-in-law made sixty-five years ago for her son—Charlie, or Winston, his penname—so I will pull it out and wash it by hand and get it ready for a picture.

A boy, a girl. It's Thanksgiving.

Blog: "Five Months"
Posted: November 27, 2008

Thanksgiving Eve, after eating at PFChang's in Cool Springs, Cory, Leah, and I stopped in at Sports Seasons, so Cory could look at Colts gear. That's when I ran across some little UT orange outfits, baby-sized . . . on clearance. Jillian Dawson, "Jillie," will have the white one with puffed sleeves and a puppy Smokey on front. Winston Hardy, "Hardy," will have the orange one with GO VOLS on his little butt. I couldn't resist, especially on the day we learned the sexes of the twin babies. Next football season, they will be wearing orange in Ole Miss/Mississippi State territory. In honor of Poppy. It was just right.

Now, it was Thanksgiving morning at six thirty, and the turkey was in, all swathed in a mixture of orange juice, orange marmalade, Jack Daniels whiskey, and fresh garlic, with lots of rosemary sprinkled on top. And I thought of something. I had no clue how to carve a turkey. In four hours I would pull that fourteen-pounder out of the oven and stare it down.

In the past when it was time to carve, Charlie would pour himself a glass of wine, roll up his sleeves, sling up his arms, and tell everybody to get out of his way. He meant it, too. The whole family would disperse to the living room and give him plenty of space. Except the dog, of course. Chaeli sat by his right leg, in hopes a piece would fall to the floor. And Cory, who had entitlement to the kitchen at all times, stood at his right shoulder, crowding him, watching, waiting for some dark meat, giving unsolicited advice.

So if we were going to have slices of turkey with our dressing and sweet potatoes, Cory had to step up to the plate.

It was five months today, Thanksgiving Day, that Charlie had his aortic dissection, and five months ago tomorrow, Black Friday, that he died.

The little orange outfits showed the cycle of life. Birth, death, it was all a natural part of life, Charlie would say. I'd just as soon have the birth part, by itself.

Blog: "Thanksgiving Comes and Goes"
Posted: November 30, 2008

Thanksgiving 2008 was now but a memory. All the shopping, planning, preparing, and cooking got consumed in an hour, even though the conversation around the table lingered. And the Carving of the Turkey went off without a hitch.

My friend Currie contributed to our dessert choices by bringing over the World's Most Beautiful & Delicious Pumpkin Pie. She used all Canadian ingredients, because that's where she's from, except for the can of pumpkin. Her filling had a hint of orange zest and was not nearly as spicy with cloves and cinnamon as mine.

The meal consisted of turkey, squash dressing, garlic mashed potatoes, oven-roasted sweet potatoes and Vidalia onions, traditional green bean casserole, and Bing cherry salad. Desserts included pumpkin pie, hummingbird cake, and pecan pie. This year, it was just three of us: me, Cory, Leah. Nobody sat in Charlie's place. I turned a wine glass upside down there, among the flowers Currie had brought, gathered from her back yard. We had a toast to the one no longer with us, then clinked our glasses to his and went on with our meal.

Because, by golly, I was determined to keep up the tradition. He would've wanted that.

Then Friday, we put up the Christmas tree.

Thanksgiving ushered in the Christmas season—when everybody was decorating, shopping, baking, and planning family get-togethers, and there was Mama, a W-person of two and a half years. She lived alone, and the nearest family was two hours away. It was hard to be alone in a season of joy, ribbons, Snickerdoodles, surprises, and blinking lights.

My sister Judi and I drove down to the Mississippi Delta, to Cleveland from Memphis and Nashville, respectively, in early December to set up a Holiday Table for Mama. We took Christmas decorations, like a painted wooden tree with bells on the branches, a snow globe, a little rocking horse with wrapped packages on its saddle, red candles, and a fat wooden Santa. We spread them all out on a card table covered with a red-and-green-plaid cloth, then put out individually wrapped nonperishable candies and cookies in silver and crystal dishes that she could sample during her long days alone.

Judi put twenty wrapped presents under the tree. Mama was supposed to open one a day and let us know what item was inside the shiny holiday paper. The gifts would last until Christmas Eve, when Todd would pick up my mother to spend Christmas with the family. Judi and I knew the instructions, but the memo didn't get out to the rest of the family, and I got a phone call from Todd.

Blog: "Mamaw's Surprises"
Posted: December 6, 2008

"What in the world is wrong with Mamaw, and why is she sending everybody a one- or two-word email every day that doesn't make sense?" Todd's faith in his grandmother's sanity was wavering. "Today it was 'Fig Newtons.' What is *wrong* with her?"

I laughed.

"Yesterday it was 'Rice Cakes.' The day before it was 'Flashlight.' I never know what to expect when I open my email."

"What about the day it was 'TRESemme Ultra Fine Mist'?"

"Or 'Bird Seed.' What has gotten into her?"

"You mean you really don't know?"

"No, I don't know. A few days ago it was 'Pizza Cutter.'"

"Your mamaw put up her little Christmas tree the day before Thanksgiving. She even bought new lights and strung them around it. She moved a rocking chair in the living room and she sits there and looks at the tree lights. Your Aunt Judi hauled in twenty wrapped presents—just little things. She arranged them all around the tree, and every day until Christmas, Mamaw is supposed to open one. And she is supposed to email us and tell us what she got. And even though we are all far away, we can celebrate with her every single day."

"Well, for crying out loud, I thought she had lost her mind."

December 11. Charlie's birthday. Time had stopped for him, so there was no counting up to another year.

December 15. The dog's birthday. Chaeli was ten. In people years, she was seventy, much older than Charlie had been when he died.

Christmas. I drove to Mississippi, just Cory, me, and the dog, to spend Christmas with Todd, his four-months-pregnant-with-twins wife, and my mother. Packing the car was a simple affair this year. It never had been before. Charlie always freaked out about space. "Don't buy any big gifts!" he'd say. And I always did. "Tell Cory to bring a small suitcase," he'd say, "and not that big duffel bag." Cory always brought the big duffel bag. "Everybody out of my way," he'd say. "I've got to figure out how to get all this stuff in the back of the car. It's way too much. It'll never fit." It always did. "It's packed to the top. I can't see out the rearview mirror," he'd say about the cargo area of the Rodeo and then the Subaru.

Todd put one of Charlie's orange UT caps on top of his Christmas tree, as I did with the tree I'd put up at home. It was a way to keep a part of Charlie with us on this first Christmas he wasn't with us. We found meaning in small acts that kept a memory of him in our daily routine.

I'd decided I wasn't going to be left out when it came to opening packages, since I didn't have a husband to buy me anything anymore, so I bought myself two gifts—black fleece pants and a teal fleece shirt from REI in Brentwood. I wrapped them and acted surprised when I opened them. "It's exactly what I wanted!"

Blog: "Six Months"
Posted: December 28, 2008

It's hard to believe that I've been without my soul mate for six months. Six months ago today, my husband died. I can still see those black curls, I can still smell him, and I still have one saved message from him on my cell phone, not that I need it to remember his deep, soothing voice. All the firsts have

come and gone, except our wedding anniversary which is New Year's Eve, and then a new year that I will enter without him.

Of all the things I miss, I guess what I miss the most are the early mornings. Charlie would be working as Winston on his blog, and I'd be in my upstairs office writing or revising an essay. Occasionally, I'd venture downstairs and plop down in the wicker chair beside his desk. He'd look up at me, take his hands off the keyboard, and say, "I guess you want to talk." Sometimes I did. Sometimes I'd say, "No, I just want to be close to you." Sometimes I'd ask him to brainstorm with me, if I needed an opinion, or if I needed a particular word to fit a particular place, or if I needed to come up with a creative phrase or title.

The dog misses his presence, too. She hates to be away from home, but was obviously happy to be in a house with lots of people and noise for Christmas. She even lay at Todd's feet and rolled over on her back, as if to say, "You can be my new Alpha. I need somebody." Lord knows I can't be the Alpha. I get her boohiney—not her face—snuggled up close to me at night.

It's too quiet and lonely at home.

Six months. Seems like this should be a significant milestone. But . . . .

My wedding anniversary—New Year's Eve—ended the year 2008. Charlie and I would've been married fourteen years. The year we got married, my kids were teenagers still living at home, but old enough to spend one night alone so we could have a one-night honeymoon. Or maybe they weren't old enough, because they each invited a friend over, and they set off fireworks inside the house. Yes, inside. On our anniversaries Charlie and I would celebrate at Valentino's on West End in Nashville. We'd have champagne, and he'd have Veal Saltimbocca, and I'd have Veal Piccata and Tiramisu for dessert.

Halfway through the first year, it hit me as I looked around my agency office at all the other employees, people I worked with and talked to daily. Charlie didn't know any of them. I'd met people he didn't know. I'd done things he didn't even know about. He didn't know my life any more. I'd sort of . . . built . . . a new life.

I remembered my sister saying the night he died, "You've got to build a whole new life."

I guessed new life just sort of sneaked up on me while I was busy and not paying attention.

One of the hardest things to do in that new life was to walk into a brand new year without my loved one, knowing life was moving on for me and he wasn't a part of it. And so 2009 came marching in, and the dark days of winter came down.

Blog: "Spring Won't Skip Its Turn"
Posted: February 15, 2009

My first daffodil bloomed early last week. Now the whole clump was bursting forth—downy yellow heads, delicate on hard cold ground.

Spring came softly.

It sneaked up on me, everywhere I turned, trees budding, birches tasseling, dogwoods getting ready to open their tiny white balls filled with crunched-up blooms. I was not ready for it. In the world I lived in, it was hard to see life coming forth all around me. I was cocooned in death, loss, grief, a world that had changed and turned harsh. I felt like the fragile flower sitting in the middle of it all. I *was* the dogwood flower crunched up like a tight fist inside its cover—it got glimpses of warm sunshine, but it stayed put for now.

When I did stick a petal out to test this new world, I got ambushed every time. Ambushes: reminders that suck your breath away.

Last Friday night I went to "A Black Tie Affair" presented by the African American Heritage Society of Williamson

County at the Embassy Suites. Their mission is to preserve their culture and foster understanding and appreciation of their heritage. The night's theme was "Change Gonna Come," honoring those civil rights activists who helped break the barriers of racial and social injustice. One of the most powerful moments was the reading of Martin Luther King's "I Have a Dream" speech. King said back in 1963, "I have a dream that . . . the sons of former slaves and the sons of former slave owners will be able to sit down together at the table of brotherhood." And we did. No doubt the men and women I sat with had ancestors who were slaves, and for certain, my great-great-grandfather Beaman Hardy owned two slaves. Change did come. It was a nice evening, and I was proud of myself for taking this big step of going out *alone.*

As I drove away at eleven o'clock, I found myself stopped at a red light at the intersection of Carothers and Cool Springs Boulevard. I got ambushed because this was the spot where ten or twelve years ago on Sunday afternoons that Charlie and I parked his Rodeo and loaded up big fieldstones that were being uncovered by new construction—stones to place around our back yard pond and flowerbeds. This place was barren then—no road, no buildings, no nothing—just a gravel inlet off the boulevard, with weeds, dirt, scraped earth, and gray rocks upturned. Now it was full of streets, shops, traffic, buildings, and hotels, and now I sat alone in my car in a long green velvet dress, wearing the silver bracelet he bought me at Jared's. Change did come.

I thought about how he should have been at this event. For years he was Manager, Corporate Minority Business Development at Alcoa Aluminum Company. He worked with Minority and Women's Business on a state and national level. He was in the White House during the Reagan and Bush One years and met Governor Clinton at a trade show in Arkansas.

Plaques and awards on the shelves in our home office told the story of all the good he did. Change did come.

In an otherwise yellow daffodil world, I was buried in taxes this week—not the normal package I prepared every year for our accountant, but two business tax versions this year—one for January 1-June 28 when Charlie was owner/operator of GENISYS and one for June 29-July 31 when I was owner by default after he died. It was bad enough last summer to have to move furniture, inventory, supplies, and peripherals he'd accumulated over the years out of the office, but now I had to physically type up and look at the list of dispositions—all _his_ things I'd had to write off, sell, store, throw away. After taxes, I'd have to fill out another form for the State of Tennessee—all the assets and liabilities he left me. Someone might as well take a knife and slide it down my forearm and let it bleed out all this data in a red stream across the floor.

And then came Valentine's Day, another Dreaded First, and the reality that there would never again in my life be red roses. I saw men in Publix buying bouquets, women perusing the card rack, and every red heart was an ambush, an arrow piercing my own heart. Change did come.

This year, instead of roses, I had daffodils. Daffodils that I wanted to stomp back in the earth. And I just wanted to know how there could be all this new and fresh life everywhere around me. Because my world was still of winter. And I wanted spring to just skip this one year and give me some time to catch up.

Blog: "Moonrise, Sunrise, New Day"
Posted: March 22, 2009

At five this morning, I watched a sliver of moon rise quickly in the southeastern sky. Moons were supposed to be nocturnal. Why was this one coming up before daybreak? Was it getting ahead of itself?

Early spring brought such urgency. I felt it when I was outdoors and aware of my surroundings, and my pulse tamped out the rhythm. The bird-songs were loud and rapid trilling, the trees were desperately pushing out buds, and flowers were coming up out of cold earth. An awakening. Yesterday the branches were bare, today they had red tassels, and tomorrow there would be lush green leaves that seemed to appear all in the twinkling of an eye. Nature pushed things forward and around in circles. Nature rushed winter to spring.

Life abounded. Robins pecked in the tall fescue. A squirrel jumped over the fence and ran across the yard, toward the patio, across the patio, to the goldfish pond, where he took a drink. Then he ran through the grass past the statue of an angel reading a book, and climbed the arbor that would soon be wrapped in white wisteria. He reached the top, scared off a bluebird, and stopped to scratch and smooth his tail.

I noticed the grape hyacinths beside the concrete statue were blooming.

The forsythias were in full colorful display—I had nine of them. The Carolina jasmine was ready to open. My back yard would be all yellow like the sunrise of a new day.

I was getting there, too.

Blog: "Full Moon"
Posted: April 8, 2009

It was about seven p.m. when my son called. My daughter-in-law thought her water broke. She described what happened.

"I think you'll be having babies tonight," I said. I'd just told my son a few days ago the babies would come by the tenth, because there was a full moon on the ninth, and everyone knows babies are born during full moons.

She went to the bathroom, then returned and announced, "My water *definitely* broke."

"Get your stuff. We're going to the hospital," my son said to her.

I went to fill my car up with gasoline so I could travel down there tomorrow. I cried and laughed. Did I eat supper? I walked around the circle to gain some calm. It didn't work.

Eight thirty p.m. They were in the birthing suite, and a nurse handed my son a gown.

Eight fifty-nine p.m. They were getting ready to go back to delivery. She'd be having a C-section. I was missing it. It came during week thirty-five, not thirty-seven, as planned. I'd hoped to be there. I went with my son through his first delivery—when Buffy had her litter of puppies. We had to break the sac on the first one because Buffy didn't know what to do. Then a few years later when our black dog Julie had her litter, my son was about eleven and with her the whole way. She decided to deliver under our workshop in the back yard, which was supported by concrete blocks, leaving a span of about twelve inches. Julie waited out the day in labor in the center of that crawl space, and my son was under from the shoulders up, with a book, reading, while she labored. He was there for her all day. I knew from that moment on he would be a good father.

Nine twenty-four p.m. No word yet. The sister-in-law was assigned to call people. "Tell her to call me first," I said. It was so hard to sit and wait. I baked dog cookies, ate M&M's, and unloaded the dishwasher. I had four phones sitting around me. I only needed one to ring. I had a headache.

Nine forty-one p.m.—a text message from the delivery room. "They're here."

That's it. I'm a grandmother. I don't feel like one. I'm a grandmother. Oh my goodness. What do I do? Cry? Laugh?

Breathe.

I'm a grandmother.

They're here!

I had nobody to tell. Nobody to share the good news with. No. Body. I looked around at my four walls. Not only was the grieving person alone in the lonely times, but she was alone in the joyful times, as well. My heart was bursting with excitement, and Poppy wasn't there to laugh and rejoice with me.

Grief is erratic.

The first year, I knew loss and new life. The first year, I wailed, whimpered, and wept. The first year, I learned to smile again in the midst of it all.

The only way through grief was going right straight through the middle of it.

Once a month, that anniversary date—the twenty-eighth— would come. Twelve times it came that first year. And each time, I had to re-live all the details of Charlie's death as the big hand on the clock ticked around in a circle.

June brought the one-year anniversary. I'd plateaued in my grief journey—still holding on some, still letting go a little. I still had a big step to take. I knew without a doubt that before the end of the first year, I had to scatter Charlie's ashes.

I learned that one year was not a magic time frame. There is a beginning point to grief, but grief does not end. It's always there. Like any wound from trauma, it heals over, but a scar remains.

You get used to being without your loved one physically. You uncouple. You learn to live on by yourself.

You learn basic survival.

You Will Always Be

I waited so long to take care of business. I just couldn't do it sooner.

He'd told me the whole time we were married: "I want my ashes put in the Tennessee River across from Neyland Stadium." I had to take a trip to Knoxville.

As time pressed on toward that first-year anniversary of Charlie's death, I sensed he was restless, ready to be released according to his wishes. "Such an adventurer needs freedom and would not fare well in captivity."

That was from his story "A Will to Live." I read it again yesterday. Charlie was writing about "seeing an empty Styrofoam cup in the center turn lane of the busy street out front. There was a push of air from heavy traffic in both directions, causing the little truncated cone to roll in an arc first one way, then the other. The occasional draft of a larger vehicle would move it up and down its chosen lane a few feet. Then more rolling in arcs around its new pivot point until another large draft moved it a few feet forward or backward." He was the cup. In those long hours after his aortic dissection, the doctors struggled to give him life and he struggled to have it, and they kept making attempts at repairs, and he kept dying, until he finally let go and found his resting place.

I also understood, after a year's groping at life, surviving, existing, pressing onward, trying to find me and meaning, that in the hours after his death, he was speaking to me through his story—because I was the cup.

I set the date for scattering the ashes. Saturday, June 27, 2009—one day before the first anniversary, the last of the Dreaded Firsts.

David drove over to Franklin from Huntingdon on Friday evening, and he rode to Knoxville with me, and Cory came from Asheville. We met in a parking lot on the University of Tennessee campus about two blocks from the stadium for that final river walk.

The first thing I had to do was take the ashes out of the Belmont urn. It had a hidden sliding bottom, supposedly for making scattering easier, but I couldn't carry that wooden box on a hike to the river. I had to do something less obvious, and besides, it was heavy.

David and Cory stood in front of the car on the sidewalk under a shade tree and talked about the drive over, jobs, and how hot it was, like men always do.

I picked up the urn from the car's back floor and set it on the seat. The ashes were inside a plastic bag with a twist tie. I opened the urn and took hold of the bag, my fingers pressing in on the soft contents like it was a bag of flour. I'd never opened the urn, I'd never looked at the ashes, and I didn't know what ashes looked like. I'd always thought it would be a fine powder, but no, there were bits of bones mixed in with the ashes, and I almost fainted. I'd never fainted, and I couldn't fall apart in front of my son and brother-in-law, so I closed my eyes to make the world stop going around.

"Are you okay?" Cory asked from the sidewalk. David looked at me, his mouth open, waiting for my answer.

"I'm fine," I said. "Fine."

I put the bag in a canvas tote, and I also took along a pair of black Reebok tennis shoes Charlie had kept at the office. He wore them when he did bench work or preventive maintenance at a customer site. I had a plan for them.

"Do you want me to carry that?" David asked.

"No, I'll carry it." This was my responsibility. I had to carry Charlie. Had to.

We walked across Neyland Drive, not talking much, not knowing where we were going, but looking for an appropriate spot.

We passed a boathouse, a restaurant, and the Vol Navy docks. We walked alongside a railroad track and under an old railroad bridge. There was a long pier that offered some privacy, and there were no people around, so we walked out on the weather-dried boards to the very end, where two iron posts stuck up out of the water. I noticed a fish smell in the air, kicked up by waters gently lapping at the bottom posts of the pier, and the sashaying of the water made it a dizzying walk. I could see the restaurant with outdoor seating westward down the way, and I hoped the diners couldn't see what we were doing. Out on the river a little further east, speedboat races were in progress, and each contestant would drive as far as our pier and the trestle bridge before circling back, so I had to do my duty between boats.

I sat down on the pier. Corey squatted, and David stood beside me. I took out the plastic bag, removed the twist tie, careful not to let it fall in the water, and squeezed my hand around the bag's midway point to keep from pouring out all the ashes because I had to save some to scatter on Charlie's mother's grave after she died. I choked out some words: "Charlie, this is what you wanted, and I'm doing this for you, leaving you here in the river by your stadium." Then I dumped half the bag of ashes into the water and watched my husband sink downward into the darkness beyond where I could see him.

"You were a good man, Charlie Rhodes."

David said he knew rivers and he knew Charlie was going straight down, that he wouldn't be floating on the river. I wanted to imagine him moving in the stream, following the boundary between West Tennessee where he was born and lived as a boy and Middle Tennessee where he lived his final twenty years, on to the Ohio River where my mother lived and played as a child, on to the Mississippi River, then down by Rosedale near Cleveland where I was born and raised and where my mother still lived.

As we stood and walked away, I turned, looked back at the cloudy, rippling water, and through a blur of tears said, "I'll always love you."

We walked back along the landscaped sidewalk following the river right across from Neyland Stadium. The bank was twenty or so feet above the water in some places and covered with rip rap, big rocks used to armor the shoreline. I stopped at a spot that was mixed with trees and rocks, and a boulder there jutted out with a perfect view of the water—the stadium on one side, the river on the other. I carefully placed Charlie's shoes there, toes pointing toward the Tennessee River. In the fall there would be more than a hundred thousand people behind him, with the noise of the Pride of the Southland Marching Band and the feverish pitch of "Rocky Top."

I retired Charlie's shoes. I got the idea from my friend Currie, who never throws old shoes away when they have outlived their usefulness. She retires them. She travels with them to a city she likes and leaves them on the bank beside a river or the ocean, toes facing the water. It's her desire for freedom, she said. Water was always moving somewhere, she said, moving toward something, the destination a mystery.

This was all so fitting. Charlie got his electrical engineering degree here on The Hill, and he loved Tennessee football. When he lived in Knoxville for five years during college and then his first job at Alcoa in Maryville, he surely saw this river every day. In this place he got the education that gave him his destination: two successful careers—corporate Alcoa Aluminum and GENISYS Systems Group. From Knoxville, the river twisted west and went by the Boy Scout camp where he served as a counselor during his high school summers. Charlie was an Eagle Scout.

David was walking ahead of Cory and me on the way back to the car. He crossed Neyland Drive, but I was hot and tired and emotionally spent, and had to stop and rest. Cory stayed with me. David veered off the sidewalk by the street, headed toward the stadium where there was construction going on, and walked right up a sidewalk to an entrance.

"Look at David. He'll do anything," I said to Cory. "He won't be able to get in there. Those doors are locked tight."

The doors were wide open. He walked right in.

A feeling of urgency rushed through me and brought fresh energy. "Let's go, let's follow him in, let's go."

We walked right in, too, and we all stood at the first level and looked down at the green field. Rocky Top. The home of the Tennessee Volunteers football team.

I couldn't let this opportunity pass.

"I need to spread some ashes here," I said.

"Go, do it." Cory took out his camera to record it.

I had to work quickly before anyone noticed we were in the stadium and ran us out. I sat down on a concrete row and fumbled opening the bag of ashes, and I had no choice but to gather them in my hand. I'd called my funeral director before coming to Knoxville, and she told me how to stand against the wind and let the ashes blow away from me and that it is traumatic for some people if the ashes blow back on them. They don't want the ashes to touch them. But this was an opportunity of a lifetime. I held as much of Charlie in my palm as I could, I walked all the way down those concrete steps, and his ashes dribbled out of the cracks of my fist as I went. I got to the edge looking out over the field. I had to make it inconspicuous in case anybody was watching, so I threw up both arms in a V, and as I did, I released the ashes, and I shouted, "Go Vols!" I watched the cloud float and drift and fall to the ground under the goalpost in front of the scoreboard.

For all time, Charlie will be right there when that player with the football tucked under his arm comes across the goal line for six points. He'll be right there on the orange-and-white-checkered border. It was serendipity.

As I stood there and took in the gravity of the moment, I saw an image of him, a cameo, there in front of me, over the field, and he was laughing. Laughing at me and what I'd just done. He never asked to be on the grass of Neyland Stadium. He'd never thought of that, I guessed, and he was pleased. The image I saw was Charlie as he looked when I met him. He had thicker, curlier black hair, narrow mustache, and a brown tweed jacket on. I guessed, for eternity, you get to pick out which age you want to be, maybe your happiest time of life on earth.

I still had Charlie on my hand as David, Cory, and I walked across campus to the Copper Cellar for lunch. It was an odd feeling, and I kept my fingers outstretched. I didn't think I should wipe my hand on my pants. But the adrenalin flowed because I was holding him. After a year of not having him, I had him. I turned and asked David if he wanted to shake my hand. He did it, but I'm not sure I made it clear why I was asking—one last chance to touch his brother. When we got to the restaurant, I went to the bathroom. I had to wash Charlie off my hands. Maybe there was some symbolism in that. It choked me up a bit, but I quickly got off those thoughts about putting my husband in the water system of the city.

Nothing could top my "high" feeling. I got to put Charlie under the goalpost in Neyland Stadium. I will always have reason to smile when it's football time in Tennessee.

Before every UT ballgame that he attended, Charlie ate lunch at the Copper Cellar, so this was a fitting tribute. Every lunch, he had a Bloody Mary, so I ordered one with the liquor on the side. I had to drive home, after all. We toasted Charlie with our teas and Bloody Mary.

And so, all you readers, everybody, please keep the toast going. If you ever go to a football game in Knoxville, or if you see an Orange Nation game on TV, whether or not you cheer for the Vols, look at the goalpost in front of the scoreboard, lift your glass of Coke or your bottle of beer, and say, "Charlie Rhodes, he was a good man!" Remember the man.

We sent Cory on his way back to Asheville, and I got behind the steering wheel of the Outback, driving David and me west toward Nashville, back to my house, where David and I would sit a while and share stories about my husband, his brother.

David talked about stopping at the outlet mall in Lebanon, if I had time.

Time was all I had.

And I felt good.

Then it hit me.

I really did feel good. I felt lighter. Had the weight been lifted? The day even seemed brighter, the colors sharper. Was this for real? Did I really feel better? Or was this just another feel-good moment that would give me a quick high, then I would crash once again to the depths of despair? Was it fleeting? What had happened?

Two lifelong wishes—Charlie's ashes in the river beside the stadium, then flowing by the Boy Scout camp—and one bonus froth-on-the-beer moment—ashes inside the stadium—had happened. These acts were not only important to the one who lost life, but to the ones left behind. Anything that honored and kept Charlie's memory going kept me going.

"Trudging through life, coping with the day-to-day challenges and turmoil, we sometimes need a reminder that we too can survive, even beyond all odds."

This was my reminder. Disposing of the ashes was the most powerful step toward healing, thus far. The releasing of him was honoring to him, and it was freeing for me. I took the remains of that man and fulfilled his request. I did something specific and physical to release what I possessed with me and in me. It put me on top of the situation and gave me power to heal.

Any time you are in a crisis, you're pushed down by it, held captive, and it has power over you. Once you rise up over it and take control in your thoughts, attitude, and actions, and do something to one-up yourself, you have power over it. That begets healing.

There is no single right way to heal. You are plucked out of life and sent on a detour down that grief road, and it's a long, bumpy walk. You get exhausted, your feet hurt, your heart pounds from exertion. The scenery is not so good either. You follow the twists and turns. You get dust in your eyes and blisters on your heels. You don't know where you are going. You don't know how you're going to get there. You don't know if you will ever get there. But you face the winds and rains and pellets of sleet, and you keep on trudging. You come to a crossroad, you make a choice, you push through safely, and the next leg of the journey is a little lighter and smoother.

I wanted this feeling to last. I was afraid it wouldn't. I was eager to see how I would feel tomorrow.

I had been to The Hill. I was "not squashed by one of the many behemoths that passed this way." I "had a nick, but was otherwise alive and well."

And Charlie got to come home to his beloved Hill where'd he now always be—HOME.

Rings, Singles, and Sapphires

"I'm not married anymore," Mama said on the day we buried Dad.

"You can think of yourself as married if you want to." I patted her on the silky shoulder of the new size eight dress my sister had to go out and buy for her to wear to the funeral. Two years of being a caregiver for my father had worn her down from a sixteen.

"No. It says 'till death do you part.'" She held her hand out, spread her fingers, and looked down at her bare third finger, left hand. "I can't wear my ring anymore."

When we got in the car after the funeral, I slammed the door on her finger. I didn't mean to, I didn't know she was holding on to the top of the car as she got in, and I hurt her in addition to the hurt she was already in. She had just buried her husband of sixty-one years, and she could no longer wear her wedding ring.

There came a time for me, too, after Charlie died, when I realized I wasn't married and should remove the wedding band. It was a hard thing to do, and I waited a long time. Those rings were my identity. They showed I belonged to someone. I was important. I mattered. Somebody cared for and about me.

There had never been a span of time in my life that I was single. I'd either been married, or engaged, or had a steady boyfriend from the time I was fourteen.

I tried removing the rings once when I went to the grocery store, and it made me feel conspicuous. I just knew everyone was staring at my hand and wondering what was wrong with me that

I didn't have a husband. I was still grieving, missing my husband, and yet insecure and embarrassed because I didn't have one. I didn't want to take my rings off.

I wore three on my third finger. Soon after our first date, my birthday came along, and Charlie went to the Service Merchandise jewelry department and bought me a gold band with a raised row of channel-set blue sapphires. I thought at the time it was a little soon for him to be buying any kind of a ring, but I accepted it. I had removed a diamond engagement ring and wedding band from my first marriage two months earlier, and my finger was bare. When Charlie and I decided to get married four months later, we declared that sapphire ring as my engagement ring, for I was already wearing it on the appropriate finger. For my wedding ring we took my dad's original band—my mother had surprised him with a new one on Christmas a few years back—and had the jeweler melt it down and make a mold in the same design as my sapphire ring. At the same time, Charlie had another matching band made with white sapphires to give me on our first anniversary.

I'd worn those three rings fourteen years. Removing the rings was symbolic of moving beyond the loss I'd experienced. When I took them off, the first segment of that third finger was white and triple-band marked. The imprint of the rings would remain for years to come—the imprint of three circles.

A circle is an unbroken line. No beginning, no end. No divisions. The perfect symbol of completeness and eternity.

The sun is a circle. The moon is a circle. They are fixed points in the sky of my life. They will never go away. If they do, my world ends. My world needs them for light, warmth, growth, stabilization as in the pull of gravity, and life.

I thought my husband gave me all these things, too.

I remembered a picture of a tree he painted in oils after a failed marriage, years before I met him. He titled it "Single." The number one is a lonely number. But the number one also represents new beginnings.

Charlie created the tree on a canvas board painted black on the bottom two thirds and white at the top. He'd made a wooden frame to attach to it and painted it black.

Black symbolizes unhappiness, sorrow, and mourning. It's the color of the night, the depths of the unknown. White means light, goodness, and successful beginnings.

The tree looked like one a child would paint—straight trunk and big round top with green leaves and a little red mixed in for contrast.

Red is the color of fire and blood, associated with strong emotions—love, strength, passion. Red signifies the color of the sun, a symbol of energy radiating life.

Now, the sun and the moon were just hanging there. Charlie was behind them. They moved across my sky and around my world, and he followed.

I was grounded here on earth.

For a tree to grow on top as big and round as the one Charlie painted, it must have an expansive root system. The roots must grow and spread out, and then the tree can fill out the top branches to equal its footing below the surface. The canopy above the ground will match the root system below the ground.

The tree had to have solid footing, and it could hold itself up.

I decided to take just the gold band off and wear the two sapphire rings.

The sapphire is the symbol of heaven. The gem draws protection and prophetic wisdom to the wearer. It oversees her divine destiny, instilling hope, faith, and joy during the journey.

I'd lost part of me, but I was still holding on to part. I was gaining my footing—learning to be single.

The ring decision was a step toward becoming a new me.

Mama

"I'm rum."

"You're what?" I pushed the phone hard against my ear till it hurt the cartilage, so I could make out the consonants and the vowel between them. "I don't know what you're talking about, Mama."

"I'm rum. You know . . ." She dragged out the short U and said it scratchy. "Ruuum."

"Mama, you've lost your words again. What does that mean?"

"Rum." She said it softer, then laughed. She was getting it, that her word confusion problem was blowing her cover as being totally competent and in control, and she tried to laugh it away. I could picture her sitting there, in her big stuffed chair we bought after Dad died, with a pillow and heating pad behind her, and on the end table beside her, eye drops, fingernail file, clear polish, salt and pepper because she ate her meals there, and a coaster for a cup of tea, Lipton Orange Pekoe. The window air conditioner would rattle on, then off. It was August and hot in Mississippi. Mama was eighty-eight.

"You're rum," I repeated and laughed.

She laughed, too. We laughed together, loud and hard, and I turned sideways on my couch, put my legs up and hugged them with my free arm, leaned my head back, and a good solid minute of laughing went by. Lord, it felt good to laugh with her and ignore everything else.

For ten years I'd talked to my mother every day on the phone. Most days, an hour. Some days, we'd talk three or four times. We were a six-and-a-half-hour drive apart, and we had to rely on phone and email to stay in touch. We managed the cost because she got a special phone company package that gave her unlimited calls to other users of the same provider for twenty-five dollars a month. If I wanted to talk, I'd ring her number one time, hang up, and she'd call me back. I got charged a few pennies for every dial and hang-up, but who was counting? At the turn of the millennium we did genealogy together by phone—the Hardys on Dad's side and her Mahaffeys and Boones from Kentucky and Ohio. She did much of the online research and ordered land and military documents, sometimes forgetting and ordering again and paying twice for the same ones, and we'd laugh about it. Then we'd just talk about anything, or nothing, really, or the same thing we'd talked about the day before. She'd tell the same stories over and over, mostly about her childhood and four brothers and five sisters, and also about her Army days. The Army days—it was just like they were yesterday. I could count on her to call every Saturday morning about nine. I'd tell her I was going out to work in the flowerbeds. I'd take the phone with me, put her on speaker, set it beside me on the ground, and pull up weeds. After half an hour went by, she'd say, "You better go on out and get your work done." I'd answer, "I already did it, Mama." So we'd talk another half hour.

I counted on those talks after Charlie died. I needed her. She was the only company I had, besides the dog. Mostly, I'd just listen to her. She had no one to talk to all day, so she was loaded and ready. To keep her words, she needed to use them in communication.

But as 2008 headed down the stretch toward 2009, the conversations started turning toward problems and pains Mama was having. Her back hurt, and her stomach hurt. "It's my colon," she'd say. "I'm constipated." The doctor said all old people worried about their bowels. It was all they talked about. The pain was taking her over, and to make matters worse, she'd forget and leave the teapot boiling away on the stove while she was off in another room folding clothes or outside planting flowers.

Now, high summer of 2009, she was "rum." I wondered what pain pills she'd taken and how many.

"She can't stay alone any more," Judi said. "She's going to burn the house down with her in it." The burden of our mother's care rested on my sister, who lived closer than I did—in Memphis, two hours up Highway 61 from Cleveland. Judi wanted our mother in a place where someone could make sure she was safe all day and all night. I wanted our mother at her own home at 807 Deering Street, and if she fell out in the back yard and died on the Bermuda grass, so be it. That would be a good thing. Just like I had wanted Dad to die in his barber shop while cutting a head of hair. I didn't mean it in an ugly way. I just wanted them to have a normal life until the end. But when the end got near, they weren't normal—they were different looking and different acting and not at all like they used to be.

And neither died the way I chose. We prayed that Mama wouldn't go the same way Dad did—of end-stage dementia, which meant starvation and dehydration, because at the end, dementia patients can't eat or drink. The bottom line seemed to be that death was death, and death was hard no matter how it came. We had to get on that road and ride it down.

I was right to want Dad to die of a heart attack with his scissors in his hand in the City Barber Shop on North Street, and I would soon know I was right to want Mama to die outside on the ground under her Carolina jasmine with the squirrels and birds she fed daily coming to see about her. A long, honorable life should end in an honorable way.

Dad was in World War II, went to Bastogne and Trier, where he got a Bronze Star with Valor and a battlefield commission to Second Lieutenant. Mama joined the Army and met Dad on the base in Georgia, exactly as a gypsy fortune teller had predicted in 1937, when Mama was sixteen. "You will travel over many waters— not the ocean, but rivers," the gypsy woman said. "You will be in uniform. You will marry a man in uniform. You will have two daughters." Mama said she just laughed at her fortune, because why in the world would she have on a uniform? Two years later, World War II broke out. Two years after that, Japan bombed Pearl Harbor, and two years after that, Mama joined the Army and traveled over many rivers to Georgia from Ohio, where she met Dad who was a Tenth Armored Tiger. She married him ten days before he shipped out with the Third Army and General George Patton. Ten years after that she had her second daughter, my sister.

Mama and Dad went to college on the GI Bill—Dad to barber college and Mama to Delta State Teachers College. She got a Bachelor of Science, double major, in social studies, with the highest average in her graduating class. She also got a BS in elementary education, an MS in special education, and an MS in Supervision and Administration. She taught school for thirty-three years and was Kappa Delta Pi. She had hobbies of ceramics, macramé, and sewing. She made most of the dresses my sister and I wore when we were little girls, and she even sewed outfits for Judi's Barbie doll. She taught tap dancing, and she played with us when we were little— badminton, croquet, and jump rope, Dutch and French.

The summer after she turned eighty-six, Mama was still mowing her own yard with a push mower, and she did the weed-eating and flower planting. Last summer, when she was eighty-seven, we hired someone to cut the grass for her, but she was out in the yard all the time working in the flowerbeds, and if the lawn man didn't show up on time, she'd crank the mower and do it herself. Thanksgiving 2008 came, and Mama begged us to let her stay home alone. We did with great guilt, but at Christmas, we made her join the family. Todd drove two hours to Cleveland from Jackson to get her. She said the car ride jarred her bones, and she refused to go to the baby shower for the expected twins in February, 2009. In April, however, she made herself go see the newborns in the hospital's NICU. She held each tiny baby, but I don't think she fully connected that these were her great-grandchildren. She was hurting and just wanted to sit with a heating pad on her back all day, watching old TV shows. She spiraled rapidly into confusion and word loss.

She was rum.

What was wrong with Mama?

She went to several doctors with symptoms of back pain, abdominal pain, constipation, and the need to constantly clear her throat. She was prescribed meds like Cipro, Claritin, Darvocet, Decadron, Flonase, Miralax, and Milk of Magnesia.

On Friday, May 1, Judi drove down to Cleveland after teaching all day and found Mama in so much pain that she took her straight to the emergency room. They were there ten hours, getting tests, with Judi specifically requesting a CT scan.

Surely, now we would find out what was wrong with Mama.

As it turned out, we would not get the full results of that scan until October 2, five months later, two days before Mama died, when we went and requested the report of findings.

REPORT: 05/01/2009 19:05
CT ABDOMEN WITHOUT CONTRAST:

Findings: Dilated fecal-filled pocket of large bowel or colon is evident just to the right of the midline . . . There is evidence of constipation throughout . . . There is minimal left basilar airspace consolidation [foreign substance in the lung] / atelectasis [collapse] . . . There is destruction of the T2 vertebral body and there appears to be involvement of the right pedicle suggesting that this is a metastatic process. No other destructive lesions are identified which raises the possibility that this is an isolated lesion unrelated to metastatic cancer, yet to be diagnosed.

CT OF PELVIS WITHOUT CONTRAST:

Findings: There are multiple phleboliths evident.

IMPRESSION: Several worrisome signs for malignancy, colon cancer, or lung cancer.

RECOMMENDATION: A PET/CT would be ideal. Alternative diagnostic studies include a contrast enhanced CT of the chest, abdomen, and pelvis. A bone scan (three-phase). Other nonradiologic studies such as colonoscopy, as well, depending on the clinical picture.

After the scan Mama got Miralax and Milk of Magnesia, plus Darvocet for pain.

And Mama kept on hurting.

She stayed in her chair with the heating pad, taking Ibuprofen with the Darvocet. She'd forget when she took the pills, and she'd take more in an hour or two. One day I told her, "Mama, if you're hurting this bad, you're going to be on morphine in a few months." I wanted to shock her and make her get up and be normal. I would come to hate myself for saying that.

She stopped driving, so she couldn't go to the grocery store any more, nor could she go to church. She was cut off from the outside world, isolated on her little lot at 807 Deering.

That house was now the enemy. Once filled with light and laughter and creativity and dance and song and kitchen smells and a yard full of flowers and tomato vines, it was now a dark place that held my mother hostage. At one time we were putting on cotton dresses and high heels and white gloves and going to Sunday School and coming home after church services to Mama's big dinners— rump roast, dirty rice, mashed potatoes with brown gravy, squash, corn casserole, green beans, and Coca-Cola cake for dessert. Now, Mama was eating white bread with zucchini and cheese toasted on it, mushy and nasty looking. She'd have apple dumplings and canned asparagus—soft food that was either too sweet or with no taste.

Judi was driving down every Friday afternoon and staying overnight, taking Mama to shop for groceries. I hired a young woman to clean Mama's house and cook lunch for her and prepare a plate she could warm up in the microwave for supper.

Mama kept getting worse.

In July, I took her to the doctor. I helped her onto the exam table covered with white crispy paper. Mama was a frail thing and all scrunched in, her arms wrapped around herself and her pain. She kept telling the doctor it was her colon.

"Pull up your shirt, Mama, and show him where it hurts. Point to it." She did as I said.

"Well, that's not your colon," the doctor said. Because of her back pain, he X-rayed her hip and after checking the film, he said, "I think we should do a colonoscopy."

"Why? Did you see something?"

He shook his head.

The colonoscopy showed diverticular disease, but they could not get the scope past forty to forty-five centimeters.

Mama kept getting worse.

Judi called a home health agency and requested an evaluation, and a social worker met with Mama in August and determined that she must be removed from her home immediately, that she needed twenty-four-hour care. Her pain intensified. Her confusion increased, she was losing her words, and her short-term memory was failing. And Mama was depressed because she was alone after losing Dad. She wanted Judi and me to come live with her. We couldn't. And she wouldn't come stay with us. And even if she had agreed to, we both worked and couldn't care for her all day.

We admitted her to a senior care unit for further evaluation. "Find out what's wrong with her," Judi ordered. She called me after she drove away.

"She's in."

I could hear the road noises as Judi headed up Highway 61. I sat at my desk at work, clutched my cell phone tighter, and listened.

"I just left her. And she's not happy. She was getting her purse, ready to walk out with me." Judi's voice was strong, a little shaky, but determined. It was a hard thing to do.

Mama was the matriarch, she had demanded to stay in her own house, and she threatened to sue us if we challenged that. She was a fighter, and everyone understood who and what she was, and we were all slow to cross her.

"'Who can find a virtuous woman?'" she used to quote to us from the Bible when we were little girls. "For her price is far above rubies." (Proverbs 31:10 KJV)

Mama called me her first night in the unit. "You come down here and get me, or I will hate you forever."

I thought Mama would always be like she used to be when she was young and Judi and I were little girls—stable, solid, spunky. She was a strong woman because she came from a famous pioneer family. Her third-great-grandfather was a first cousin of Daniel Boone.

She still carried the spirit of the brave girl who grew up in an antebellum house, once a station on the Underground Railroad, on a bank of the Ohio River near Cincinnati. Mama played in the river and once climbed onto a tugboat with her sister and stole a sack of cookies, got chased by the crew, and jumped off the boat into the river. Big chocolate cookies floated around her. She watched the river flood in 1933. The evening before, her mother had told her to go to the basement and get a jar of corn relish. She decided to play the Blind Game, in which she would retrieve the item in the dark, but as she lowered one foot to the first stair, a musty odor hit her in the face, and she heard a lapping noise, and something made her stop and turn the light on. There was muddy river water up to the top step. If she had run down those stairs in the dark, she would have been pulled into the rising waters and lost in the moving current. I always knew it was God who saved her.

God saved her then, but now she was this ill, withered woman at eighty-eight, the facets of her life out of her perimeters and floating around her like those big chocolate cookies.

"I don't belong here," she said, fussing about the senior care unit. "Tomorrow, you come get me."

But the senior care unit did a thorough job of examining Mama and taking care of her. They took her to other facilities in other towns for tests to find out what was wrong with her. Then they took her to an appointment with a specialist to learn the test results, and Judi met her there. The doctor put a picture of Mama's lungs on the X-ray box and made a big circle in the air with his hand to show how extensive the radiological finding was. "Your mother has lung cancer."

It was the first time we'd heard this diagnosis. Judi cried, and the doctor had to run out to get tissues for her. Mama, who didn't hear well, saw the urgency around her, but was not aware of what had been explained.

"I was the one to tell her she had cancer," Judi said. "The doctor wasn't going to do it. He thought she wouldn't understand. She was surprised and shocked. I thought she had a right to know. I refused to hide anything from her. She wanted to know how to treat it. I had to tell her with pain medication and breathing treatments. I told her no chemo because it would make her memory worse. Telling her no treatment was probably the worst minute of my whole life. We sat, and I cried. She held my hand and told me to be strong and it was past time for her. She was teary and her voice was wavering. She dabbed at her eyes with a tissue."

Lung cancer. How did my mother get lung cancer? She smoked cigarettes as a young woman, but it was fifty years ago that she threw her last cigarette out the car window on her way to teach school. After that, she could never stand to be near the smell of smoke again.

Back pain. Had the cancer spread? We wanted a bone scan.

The doctor set it up for August 28 at the Cleveland hospital. I took her for the procedure, sat in the room, and watched the outline of her little body appear on the monitor. I saw places light up, but I didn't understand what I was seeing, and I trembled inside. The following week the doctor called and told us there was uptake, which signaled malignancy. The cancer had metastasized.

Judi busied herself making arrangements for permanent care for our mother, while I glided around in a wispy fantasy that Mama could still stay at home. Truth is, I couldn't bear any more change. My whole life had been pinched to one tiny freckle that sat on the

111

top of my skin. I existed outside the circulation, heartbeat, and live tissue. Mama was a foundational rock wall of my life, and that wall was crumbling. There was nothing I could do to scrape up, push back in a pile, and cement back together the powdery chips that were sloughing off.

Mama liked the young woman I'd hired to come in the mornings and help with the house and meals, but she refused to let the home health caregiver, who came for the afternoons, inside. The woman would knock at the back door, and Mama would look out the window and say, "You go away. I don't want you here." It finally became obvious to me that it just wasn't going to work. The state home for veterans was the best option, and they had an opening September 1.

Blog: "Out, Out Blue Spot!"
Posted: September 3, 2009

It was Thursday, and the little blue mark on my thumbnail was fading.

I first noticed it through a blur of tears Sunday morning when I put my hands on the steering wheel at ten and two and headed north up Highway 61. The road was straight and flat ahead of me, tall signs and neon flashing red. I had been crying aloud and begging for answers since I said goodbye to my mother and drove away from Deering Street and the house of my childhood. How do I leave the home I grew up in? How do I leave my mother, knowing I won't see her standing at the front door waving ever again?

On Monday morning my mother would be leaving her home of sixty years. My sister would be driving her to the state VA home between Cleveland and Memphis, where she'd have around-the-clock help and palliative care. Only my mother didn't know that yet. I'd spent four days trying to assure her that we would make sure she had twenty-four-hour care and

we'd always be there for her. I couldn't even assure myself that things would be okay.

While visiting her, when I could catch some private moments, I'd wash her clothes and label them with her initials with a blue fine-point Sharpie, and I got blue marks on my fingertips and on the nail of my thumb. I'd pack the clothes in a black suitcase, and with every item I lay in a stack, I'd sob, "Please, God, forgive me." And I knew I'd never forgive myself. I was packing up my mother's things so she could go to a nursing home against her will.

Even with me in the house right beside her, Mama overdosed on her pain medications and put two patches of memory medicine on because she didn't remember that one had already been placed. She warmed up her leftover Captain D's catfish in a skillet and got involved with another task and left the eye of the stove on, and the fish burned, and the smoke alarm went off.

It was time to put safety first.

For my heart, it would never be time.

The blue spot might fade from my fingernail, but it will never go away from my heart.

Mama got a private room at the VA because she was in hospice care. But she could still socialize. She dressed up every day and walked the halls and talked to the male veterans and visited with one other woman vet. The first visit I made down there, she wanted to introduce me, and as we approached the other woman's wheelchair, Mama looked back at me and asked, "Are you my sister or my daughter?"

Blog: "Journeys"
Posted: September 7, 2009
Sunday before Labor Day at ten of six I embarked on a journey south under moonlight. I'd always wanted to take

a trip in the country under a full moon. The Natchez Trace stretched out before me in curves, over hills—asphalt, grass, a treeline. The road narrowed ahead, and an occasional leaf dropped in front of me. I didn't see another car for the first fifty minutes. I watched the sky lighten and the morning clouds burn away. A coyote crossed the road, then another, a deer, bands of wild turkeys, vultures on the center line, a hawk flying toward me, then lifting. The rising sun helped to clarify the world around me. It filtered through the trees and threw its light across the road and lay stripes against the tree trunks. Against the texture of blue-green pine needles, the hardwoods were paling, thinning, and there was a smattering of yellow. Dogwoods were turning red. Sycamores looked like succotash. They signaled the change to come. Soon winds would whip the dropping leaves across the roadway and into the fields, and there would be cold air and earthy colors, then icy rain and barrenness—the end of the living season.

Bagworms hung on branches, some out over the roadway in my path, snuffing out the life of the tree. I didn't want to experience this ugly invader on my journey through pristine woods, but I was forced to look at these obstacles in my path.

I followed the Natchez Trace to Tupelo, then took Highway 6 west. Mama had been at the VA home for six days. For now, she needed heavy pain medication and management. She was on morphine.

Mama's lung cancer had not only metastasized to the bones, but to the space between the lungs, and she had adrenal cancer, as well. Her pain was getting stronger. She couldn't stand any clothes touching the bones in her low back and thoracic area or against her ribs in front. She had made cuts into the waistbands of all her pants to allow for more room. She said a chaplain told her she had three or four months.

I was unable to cope with her impending death because I could not get past the fact that she was in a nursing home. She was in pain, she was overdosing, she was unsafe at home, she finally got her diagnosis, and she got put in another town one hundred twenty miles away, in strange surroundings, among strangers. No one would visit her there, except close family, once a week. No one from her hometown or from the church where she'd been a member for sixty-three years could come the distance to visit.

My head told me she was getting the care she needed.

My heart told me she needed to be at home. Home, where she could look out the front window and see Iva Lou's old house and two big trees in the front yard, even though Iva Lou and Carey were in North Cleveland Cemetery on the row across from Dad. Home, where she could spend her days wandering about the weigelas, roses, hydrangeas, crape myrtles, and Carolina jasmine. Home, where she could spend her last nights in the front bedroom where she had slept for sixty years. Home, where she could get peace, comfort, and closure. And die in the same room my father did.

We decided to take her home before the end. She hoped it would be soon enough. So did I.

I'd started a journey through grief after Charlie died. I'd been through the rough waters, the rapids, the rushing whitewater pulling me down the river. I had just pulled in to calmer waters. I was beginning to laugh and experience life again and to want more out of life.

Now this with Mama. And the familiar journey began again. I recognized that tingling in the backs of my arms, the heaviness of my legs as I tried to put one foot in front of the other and walk, the shallow breaths I was forced to take, and the head pointed down, chin on collar bone—the posture of grief. My pain centered in my neck, and I was drawn to the bottle of Ibuprofen, and it didn't help.

Once again, I was swept away by the current. I needed to remember to paddle.

Mama, in recent years, had been drawn back to her days in the Army. She was always asking me, "Did I ever tell you I saluted the president?" So I wrote a story for her and titled it "Mama Saluted the President." Then I condensed it to two pages, inserted a picture of Mama in her uniform, put it in two big, black frames, and gave it to her for Christmas a couple of years back. When she went to the VA home, I took the story frames and put them in her room so everybody would know how important Mama was. Sure enough, the staff read the story and made plans to get Mama on the local TV news on Veteran's Day coming up in November. They hoped, too, they could get her on CNN. She had quite a story. Not every soldier got to salute the president.

Mama Saluted the President

Mama had joined the Women's Army Auxiliary Corps in January of 1943. The WAAC was the predecessor to the Women's Army Corps, but the women soldiers didn't have military status. The WAACs were needed overseas, but the Army couldn't provide them protection, if captured, or benefits, if injured. In March of 1943, Congress opened hearings on converting the auxiliary unit into the Women's Army Corps, which would've made the women part of the Army with equal pay, privileges, and protection. It would also make a much larger army and let the women take over some of the jobs men were doing, so the men could go fight.

Mama was stationed in Ft. Oglethorpe, Georgia, the Training Center for the Women's Third Army Corps. She had volunteered for Cooks and Bakers School because she came from a family of ten children and she thought she'd be good at cooking for a crowd.

She was issued all the corps' uniforms, but the cooks wore white short-sleeved dresses when they worked.

On April 17, 1943, Mama was in cooking school wearing her white uniform. A parade was scheduled on the post that day. The soldiers were expecting somebody important, a high up, but they didn't know who it was. Mama was hoping for the president. She asked her instructor for permission to go, and her teacher said yes, and told her to put on her Army overcoat and button it all the way up to her neck to cover every inch of the white uniform.

Everybody else was already gathered at the parade grounds. As Mama ran out of the training center and down the sidewalk, a cannon began to fire, announcing the arrival of the guest. She counted the shots. 1, 2, 3. She got to the end of the sidewalk. 4, 5, 6. She ran down the steps. 7, 8, 9. She neared the street. 10, 11, 12. The cannon blasts kept coming.13, 14, 15. She saw a black car approaching. 16, 17, 18. She stopped at the curb. 19, 20, 21. She froze. Twenty-one shots. That's HIM!

The President of the United States of America was in the black open-air vehicle coming right at her. She collected herself and did what she was trained to do. She stood at attention, straight as a board. She saluted. She had to get the salute exactly right, at the tip of the hat. She knew to hold it until it was returned.

The car stopped right in front of her. President Franklin D. Roosevelt sat in the back seat of the convertible, close enough for her to put her hand down and touch him. She looked right into his eyes. His dog Fala, a Scottish terrier who could curl his lips into a smile, was sitting in the President's lap. Colonel Oveta Culp Hobby, the female director of the women's corps, was sitting beside the president. They both saluted Mama.

The president wore a black cape, and his face was white as snow. He smiled at Mama and said, "That was good, soldier."

That day, President Roosevelt reviewed three thousand WAACs on the parade grounds at Barnhardt Circle and inspected the women's training program to determine for himself whether they should become part of the Army. On July 3, 1943, three months later, he signed the bill into law, and the Women's Army Corps was born.

Mama was most likely the first soldier the president inspected on the post that day. I think Mama was the reason the auxiliary unit became the Women's Army Corps.

Mama wasn't just any another female resident there at the veterans' nursing home. She had worn a uniform, saluted the president, and made history. But now she was fighting the staff and defying orders when they tried to help her change clothes or take medicine or sit in the common area. I was visiting her the day she gave up her fight. I'd helped her into bed and asked two of the staff to change her out of her slacks into a loose gown because the elastic was hurting her. She was slapping at them, and then all of a sudden she slammed her hands to the sheets and released a breath. "Oh well. I just don't give a . . . ." and she said the word. Mama, mother, virtuous woman, first grade teacher, principal, Sunday School teacher, paragon of a woman. Those were the last words I ever heard my sweet mama say.

She had more pain and more morphine after that.

I returned to visit Mama toward the end of September and walked into the VA home before lunch, when everyone was sitting out in the common area. I looked around and didn't see my mother. I kept looking until I saw someone in a wheelchair, all skinny and hollow and hunched over, mouth wide open, and there was a look about her that said she could have been my mama.

"Ma-ma," I said and choked out the second "ma" in a sob.

All I could think of was the picture I had of my little family back in 1950 shortly after I was born—Dad in a suit and tie, me in a pale pink dress and booties. And Mama. I clearly had Mama's smile and Dad's blue eyes. Mama learned to tint pictures back then in a day of black and white. My baby face was pink and fresh. And so was Mama's. Her hair was dark brown, thick, coarse, curly, and her eyes were brown and full of happiness. She wore a dark suit with a pale pink scarf wrapped around and puffed up in the V-neckline of her jacket. Her hand touching my pink sock was smooth and young. Mama was beautiful.

Would I remember her that way, or would I remember Mama in the wheelchair in the nursing home?

I called my sister and told her Mama needed to go home now. Judi drove down the next day to see for herself. "We're going home," she said to our mother.

Judi took the Family Medical Leave Act because she worked for a large school system. I worked for a small company, so I took all my vacation and sick days to go be with Mama. Then I just wouldn't get paid. If I was gone too long, I was told I might be replaced.

September turned into October, and by Friday morning the second, we were coming unglued because of the shape our mother was in.

"I'm. So. Mad." My sister clenched her fists and hammered them against the soft pink living room couch, accenting each word she squeezed out. "It's just not right." She cried out loud as she talked. "I took her to the doctor. How many times did I miss work to take her to different doctors? I even took her to the emergency room because I didn't know what else to do and she was in so much pain. We were there till three in the morning! Why didn't they find anything then?"

I sat across the room, my legs crossed, and I swung one of them and twitched my foot up and down. My sister never cried. She never let on when anything upset her. She was the strong one. I was the emotional and sensitive one.

Our mother lay in the next room in a rented hospital bed, her head thrust back, her mouth gaping. She was not responsive.

We did not know that she was two days from death.

I was the grief veteran here. It was fifteen months earlier that Charlie had died.

"Judi, you're a victim. I'm a victim. When something like this happens that we have no control over, we are victims. We sit here while life stomps us into the ground." My chest throbbed, and I held back my tears for her sake. "You've got to get on top of it. If you think she was treated wrongly, DO SOMETHING. Take yourself out of the victim role and do something about it."

She stood and marched toward her purse. "She's had this cancer a long time. I remember us going to a doctor years ago and her complaining of a phlegm problem then. Years ago. I remember the doctor taking a spit sample. I believe she got nose spray and a decongestant. I'm going to get the records. You call and tell them I'm coming." And she was out the door.

"Okay." I first checked on my mother and swabbed her lips and inner cheeks with lemon glycerin. Then I ran to the phone book, located the number, and punched the buttons.

"My mother was a patient there several years ago. Her name is Lucille Hardy. My sister is on her way to your office. We have durable power of attorney, and we want a copy of her records. If you don't have time to make copies, stand my sister in front of the copy machine, give her the file, and she is quite capable of doing it. She's been a teacher since 1975. We need the records today."

My sister called an hour later with copies of the file in hand. "I'm stopping to get a copy of her CT scan, too, from five months ago."

An hour later Judi came in the back door crying and slammed the report down on the faux-wood kitchen countertop. "It's all here. They suspected cancer back on May the first."

Now, it was 5:00 p.m. on Friday, October 2, and I held the Radiology Report with the date and time of 05/01/2009 19:05 on it and read for the first time information that, if expressed, addressed, and heeded, probably would not have saved my mother's life, but could at least have given her comfort and the family peace during her end months.

"Impression: Several worrisome signs for malignancy . . . lung cancer. Recommendation: A PET/CT . . . a contrast enhanced CT of the chest, abdomen, and pelvis. A bone scan."

Why, oh why, just why weren't we told?

Saturday morning, I stood in the hallway looking in on Mama. There had been nothing but silence, but then she drew her legs up, knees bent, a pained expression came over her face through all the morphine, and she squeaked out, "Oooooh." Then her color changed. She turned brown that afternoon.

Sunday, October 4, ten minutes after midnight, Mama died. I lay next to her in the bed and held her hand. I told her I was sorry it all happened the way it did.

The deputy coroner got there, and we sat in the living room and waited for the hospice nurse to arrive from Yazoo City.

"Who gets the dog?" he asked, looking at my cocker spaniel.

"She's my dog," I said.

After the nurse checked Mama, she poured all the leftover morphine down the kitchen sink, while the deputy coroner and I watched.

Monday morning at eight, October 5, Judi and I went to another office and got copies of Mama's file. We did not tell anyone our mother was dead. We rushed out to the parking lot and scrambled through the pages.

"Here it is, here's the CT report from five months ago," I said.

Then we drove to Mistlow Gardens to pick out flowers for Mama's funeral.

We were angry and hurt and wanted to lash out and hurt someone else. Someone should have told us the results of Mama's scan. Nobody should ever fall through the cracks like Mama did. She shouldn't have had to go through the horrific pain of cancer— deep, persistent bone cancer pain—for half a year with little more than Ibuprofen. We approached an attorney, who would take our case only if he thought he could win, and he said Mama was old and she would have died soon anyway. It didn't seem to matter how Mama was treated.

On the day of Mama's visitation, the family began to gather at her house. I was standing in the kitchen in the same spot as when Judi had burst through the back door and slammed Mama's test results on the counter. The phone rang. It was the pathologist who examined Mama.

"I don't have all the answers yet," she said, "but I can tell you how your mother died. She had a massive embolism in her lung. She also had fecal infarction. Her intestines exploded, and there was fecal matter everywhere." There was a mass in Mama's lung.

Mama's final examination revealed a massive pulmonary thromboembolism, bronchopneumonia, bronchio-alveolar carcinoma of the left lung, right adrenal adenoma, and severe fecal impaction.

Blog: "Mama"
Posted: October 6, 2009

Visitation for Mama was tonight. Judi and I went to the funeral home this morning and set out pictures and added special touches to the room.

Mama was the solid rock of our family. The house was not the same without her. I felt the balance of my world shifting, and I liked it much better when I was the young mother with babies, and I had a mom who would be with me forever, and I had a grandmother who was healthy enough to walk the wooded paths on the family land in Kemper County.

Mama's funeral is tomorrow. Afterward, I will drive away from Cleveland, and it will never be the same. I will come back again a few times to take care of business, but this town, this place that is so much a part of me, will be lost to me—forever lost.

And so now, I was rum. You know, ruuuuum.

I felt like I was standing in front of a target, and arrows were zooming at me, but these sharp-pointed arrows were really thoughts and lessons learned, and they pierced me. Illness and disease processes change people. The strongest become the shriveled weakest, and then they disintegrate and die. One thing you do or don't do could cause somebody to die. Life doesn't give you what you want. Life doesn't let you choose the method of death. Society doesn't like old people. Old people have no worth, no value, because all they do is act weird and talk about their bowels, and they are wrinkled and repulsive, and nobody wants to touch them.

And so knowing this, how do I grow old? I already want to wrap up, cover up, and not let anybody look at me. I want to be alone, and I don't even want to say anything for fear it will be perceived as inappropriate. And in the time period between now and when I really am old, how do I deal with what happened to Mama?

What would I do in this place of the compound fracture of loss—Mama and Charlie? All those splintered pieces of information, too little information, no information, miscommunication, delays, tests and diagnoses, and wrong diagnoses. Even I let them both down. How do I process every step to destruction and come to a resting place about this in my mind?

Some of the simple folk might say it was her time, and it was God's will.

I would answer: it is not ever God's will for any human to be mis-treated—and mistreated—as Mama was. My golden retriever with cancer was given more compassion and care than my mama was early on in her disease. At the very end, Mama did get spot-on care. But it took a long time for her to get a correct diagnosis and palliative treatment.

I would also say: sometimes there is no reason. Life is random, and stuff happens. Situations spin out of control, people are dropped through the cracks, and old people don't matter. And that makes me rum.

I was a part of Mama's mis-treatment—and mistreatment—because I trusted others who were supposed to know better. We should all ask why a whole lot more, we should demand to see firsthand any reports of findings, and we should not take the word of any professional in charge of our care or our loved one's care. That, too, makes me rum.

With that understanding, I'll try to dwell in the present or look way back to the past when Mama had dark hair and happy eyes and tap danced in the kitchen, or even when Mama was eighty-seven and mowed her own grass. I'll try to avoid thinking about when Mama was eighty-eight and rum and done wrong.

Bad Things Come in Threes

Bad things come in threes, I'd always heard. After going through three significant deaths in three years—father, husband, mother—I believed it. Now it appeared that 2010 was bringing that piece of prophetic wisdom to pass with yet another group of threes: letting go of my house, losing my new job, and selling my mother's house.

It was so comforting to be in my house on Wimbledon Circle, safe in the familiar walls Charlie and I had built into a home, that I'd let a year and a half go by. I'd lived here almost as long as I lived at 807 Deering, my growing-up home I left when I was twenty.

Late on a cold February night, I turned the bed covers back and clicked on the electric afghan I'd bought Charlie for Christmas three years earlier to use in his TV-watching chair. We kept the thermostat low in the winter, on sixty-one, and he'd sit there with a jacket on. He never did use the afghan, but I got it out after he died and put it on the bed between the blanket and the spread. On winter nights like this one, it kept me toasty. I pushed my legs down toward the heat, pulled up the covers, and gave the dog a pat. I looked forward to going to bed every night, and the dog did, too. The news was on TV, and then I'd watch an episode of Barney and Andy or maybe read a few pages. This was the best time of the day. It was the only time of the day when I felt soothed.

I slept well here in this room, this house. Most people can't sleep at all after losing a spouse, but not me. There were nights when I never woke up at all, even to go to the bathroom. That had never happened, not in all my life. Every night, I watched the clock for ten to come, when I could crawl into bed and let Charlie's spirit hold me to sleep.

But I'd put off selling this house long enough.

Reality was that the mortgage payment was too high. I needed to downsize, I needed no house payment or one half the size of this one, one I could afford the rest of my life when my only income would be social security. Besides, the house and yard were too much to maintain. I knew I'd need a new roof soon, and other things would fail and need replacing.

I was under siege by squirrels. They had tried to break into an upstairs bedroom. They chewed up the outside sill. They also chewed a hole in the siding at the apex of the roof. I bought a trap, caught a few and took them to the river at the edge of the neighborhood where there were lots of trees. I borrowed a BB-gun and planned to sting the others and scare them away, but my first shot went right through the head of one and killed the little creature on the spot, and I was upset for days. I was grieving lives lost, and I took a life.

Chipmunks were overrunning me, too. They tunneled across the yard, dug around the goldfish pond, dumped dirt into the water, and stopped up the pump. Twice, they did that, and it cost me a lot of nasty work and a new pump. I spent five hundred dollars on a wild-animal-removal man, but the chipmunks kept coming. I gave up and dug out the pond and installed an in-ground stone fire pit. I was frazzled.

So I did what my husband's trusted friend advised me to do four days after Charlie died. I contacted a realtor. I was working and earning adequate money, it was W-2 income, which loan companies liked because taxes were already taken out, and I looked good overall for being approved for a loan.

One thing about me: I'll drag something out for a long time—thinking, planning, and worrying about it—and then the urge will pop into my head to do it, and I will act on it fast.

The 2010 housing market was bleak. Home prices were dropping, there was a foreclosure epidemic, and the job market was dim. One in seven mortgages was either past due or in foreclosure. One in four homeowners currently owed more on their mortgage than the property was worth. The national unemployment rate was ten percent. It was a buyer's market.

It wasn't a good time to sell.

Housing prices had skyrocketed after Charlie and I purchased so I had plenty of equity and no worries of making money on the sale. It was a matter of how much money. I needed a workable balance—a good deal and a low interest rate on a new house and a not-too-low sales price on mine.

I didn't know that at the same time I was sending a query email to the realtor, forces were in place to put all my plans in jeopardy. Shortly after I clicked Send, my supervisor at the agency told me we'd lost our biggest client, and more than half of us would lose our jobs. Those of us who didn't lose our jobs immediately would take pay cuts, and if the ones left couldn't get a new client in a couple of months, the agency would shut down.

I was the income earner of my household, and all the bills rested on me, but by now, I'd had so much loss in such a brief period of time that I was numb to it. It fell hard on me, though, that I hadn't gone home to take care of my mother during what turned out to be the last three months of her life just to keep this job.

I sat at my desk in the plush office, with its frosted entry doors, colorful art work on the black wall behind me, and red leather chairs in the reception area. My heart was thumping, yet somehow deep under the surface panic, there was a calm, because I knew it could be a good thing. I was comfortable, though not happy, in this job. I'd already had too much of an upheaval in my life, so it would take an outside force to make me leave it. I set my fingers on the keyboard and tapped out an email to my friends, sister, and sons:

"It's official. I don't know when . . . maybe today, maybe next week. I'm losing my job. We all are. Our biggest client just pulled out, and it would take a huge new client and a miracle, and that's not happening. So this changes everything for me. It's a bleak economic climate and not many businesses are hiring. I was going to put my house on the market and buy a smaller one. Now, I don't know what I'm going to do. I may have to go live in Mama's house. I may need to move . . . wherever the job prospects are, that's where I will need to go. I have a mortgage, insurance, and other bills, and I will need to act quickly. I may make a wrong decision, but I will have to make the best decision I can in the moment."

Cory wrote back: "Keep your head up. Don't let this time period get you down while you hunt for the next step. You will land on your feet. Look at my life. This has happened to me twenty times. Just don't let life slip away during this time. It counts. Stay positive, if you can. You are not alone. Doors always open."

Friday morning of that week, I cleaned out my desk and put personal things in a bag to take home. My cell phone rang. It was Mark, the realtor I'd contacted to list my house. He wanted to meet with me and get the ball rolling.

"I've got to postpone this," I said. "I'm sitting here right now waiting to lose my job." I couldn't buy a house without an income.

I got up and walked around the office, usually frenetic, now idle, people leaning over cube walls talking to each other, then some silence and shoulder shrugs. Our human resources person called us by name, and a half dozen of us went into the conference room together for our farewell speech.

A half hour later I sent another message to friends and family. "OK. It's done. I'll be leaving shortly. There are six of us leaving today. Another few next week. There are four or five staying for now."

"Go to the unemployment office," Judi answered.

"I will," I replied. "I'm getting a little severance till the end of the month, so I will go fill out paperwork early next week."

"Talk about having the rug pulled out from under you!" my friend Currie said. "Don't panic. Let the dust settle. This might just be the next phase of your life beginning. This could be leading you to doing something with writing, editing."

I knew I could make it financially. On top of unemployment and my GENISYS supplement, I'd have to rely on savings, though, which was supposed to get me through until the end of my life. I'd always had a fall-back plan. It involved Mama's house at 807 Deering Street in the town where I grew up. I could go there, redecorate, paint the white cottage dark beige, add new shutters, remodel the kitchen, expose the original hardwoods, plant crape myrtles, build flower gardens out on the sides to make it look bigger—I'd done it in my head a thousand times—and live out my days there like Mama and Dad and die in the front bedroom. I shared my plan with family, initiating an email thread of advice:

Judi: "I've always said you could buy out my half and live there. You'd have it paid off once your house sold. You could get a job at the hospital or college. Write. Still do your online stuff."

Cory: "Could take the shiny new kayak you bought down the sewage ditches and catfish ponds. LOL."

Me: "I'm just screwed, huh? There's nothing good anywhere."

Cory: "Don't give up."

Judi: "You can be like Scarlett O'Hara and go home to Tara."

But "Tara" had a FOR SALE sign in the front yard. Right in the spot where I used to do cartwheels. Or lie in the Bermuda grass and wait for the first star to appear at dusk. Right near the curb where my boyfriend would park after a date to say good night, with Iva Lou on the opposite side of the street standing in the yellow light of her kitchen window, and Judi on our side of the street stalking up the hedgerow with a flashlight to spy on me. I feared that any day now, the house status could change to SOLD.

Then not only would I be grieving for Mama and Charlie, but I'd also grieve for the house at 807. I'd be saying goodbye to my lifetime home. One thing that is wrong with me is that I think too much. I worry. I make inanimate objects animate. I grieve not only people, but houses and cars and things. I put a lot of effort into planning for hurt and loss and build up to it, escalating the pain in my mind.

Blog: "Farewell, Dear Solid House"
Posted: January 23, 2010

I remembered the summer of 1960, when Mama told me I had to read a story that I didn't pick out at the library myself, and what I had to read wasn't even a book yet. It was just a stack of papers.

Mama brought home a manuscript written by one of her professors at Delta State that would soon be published by The MacMillan Company in New York. Evelyn Allen Hammett was the Head of Languages and Literature at the college, and she wrote a story based on the diary pages kept by her eighth-great-grandmother who in 1635 at the age of eight moved from Dorchester, Massachusetts, to a new settlement on the Connecticut River. The teacher knew Mama had a little girl, and she asked Mama if I could read the book and let her know if it was age appropriate for me, a fifth grader, or if it needed to be for older junior high kids.

Priscilla, Miss Hammett's ancestor, planned to write in her journal every day on the trip to the new land. But before she left, she said goodbye to her old house. She looked about her at this house her father had built when they arrived in the new country—a solid house made of logs chinked with wedges of wood and clay, a roof of birch bark shingles, a door of bark and leather hinges, a puncheon floor of white pine, and a great stone fireplace as wide as the room and tall enough for her father to stand up in. She took out her goose quill pen and ink made of swamp maple bark boiled with a little copperas, and she wrote the first page of her journal.

She ended the entry with a house blessing. "Farewell, dear solid house. God bless the roof. God bless the floor. God bless the oven and the door."

As I held a slew of Miss Hammett's typed pages in my ten-year-old hands, I didn't know it, but in fifty years I would once again pick up these words inside a hardcover book. My mother would find a used one at a Friends of the Library sale and buy it for me. On the front, *I, Priscilla*, author Evelyn Allen Hammett. I would open it and read once again: "Farewell, dear solid house." It is a time when I will be saying farewell to my own dear solid house at 807 Deering Street. I will begin to sob softly, and my crying will swell into wailing. *To wail: to utter a prolonged, mournful cry, usually high-pitched or clear-sounding, as in grief or suffering.*

In fifty years my mother will die, and my father will have been dead for three years. In fifty years the house at 807 will pass into the hands of my sister and me, and we will give away or sell its contents, taking what we deem valuable because it is a memory. We will put a For Sale sign in the front yard. And though I will live through divorce and death and experience devastating losses, this will be about the hardest thing I will ever do because it represents the greatest loss—it is home. It is the constant in my life, the fixed point in my universe. I was brought to this house as a newborn, I will grow up here, my dead pets will be buried in the back yard, graduation gowns and a wedding gown will hang in a closet. It is the house I will always come home to, the house I will bring my babies to, and my grandchildren. I will always know that I can come here and feel safe and secure. Here, all is right with the world.

When I sign on the line to give up my lifetime home, I will not be able to do it with dry eyes. I will walk through its rooms one last time. I will touch each wall of white paint and knotty pine. I will stand in its kitchen and still see Mama standing over the white stove. I will stand in the dining room where we have eaten big Sunday dinners, the living room with its white lace curtains Mama made, the "piano room," with the upright Mama antiqued white, the hall with the floor furnace where I sat on cold nights, and my bedroom where sunshine has come through window blinds and glow-in-the-dark stars have shone down from the ceiling.

I will walk through its back yard where roses and zinnias and morning glories have grown, where pecan and walnut and fig trees have stood, where tomatoes and squash and beans have been picked from vines, where sandboxes and swing sets and sliding boards have stood, and where children have made mud pies and played badminton and croquet and hide-and-go-seek. I will see the old hedges that surrounded the house, the ones that Dad trimmed every Monday because he was a barber and needed to cut something, and I will even remember the "stickers" on little weeds that blew into the back yard one year after a Texas windstorm and caused me to no longer be able to go barefooted in the Bermuda grass.

Farewell, dear solid house. God bless your roof. God bless your floor. God bless your oven and your door.

My cell phone rang me back to reality on this cold February day, as I pulled into the Publix parking lot to stock up on food because the paychecks were ending. The call was from a Mississippi prefix—the realtor for Mama's house.

"I have great news for you. I have two contracts on your mother's house."

"Of course you do. Just when I was about to move back there and live in the house myself because I lost my job."

The higher offer was a cash amount. My sister and I accepted.

Gone would be my lifetime home and my backup plan.

Blog: "The S-words"
Posted: February 6, 2010

I was finally understanding myself. I came up in a safe world, the prosperous post-war years, in a small town where everyone knew me. No parents in the world were more stable than Ray and Lucille Hardy. They bought their little white house after the war and barber college in 1949 and died in its front bedroom in 2006 and 2009, respectively. I grew up with STABILITY and SECURITY.

No wonder I had a hard time with change. When I left my daddy's home, life gave me change. Every few years, I moved, jobs changed, houses changed, children came, children left. Then a gnawing feeling in my gut grew stronger. I wanted to put down roots. I wanted to stay somewhere for a long time, for the rest of my life. I wanted what my parents had. I wanted stability and security.

This week marked the fifteenth anniversary that I'd lived in the house Charlie and I built.

I was finally realizing, however, that life was not made of stability. Life was dynamic. It was filled with choices. I could make changes if I wanted to, but most of the time, I chose not to. But then there were those changes that came unexpectedly, that just flat knocked me off my feet and pulled the ground out from under me. I had no choice. I was in a whirlwind, and I was caught up for the ride of my life. I groped for solid ground to fix my feet on, and it was not there.

There was no such thing as security. People were torn away from me, jobs, even houses that fit around me and sheltered me. I could plan, I could surround myself with what I needed to be settled and secure, I could have everything worked out for the rest of my life, and it was guaranteed that all of it would be ripped away, too. In all likelihood, the best laid plans would not follow the intended track.

So I will plan, but I know it won't last and so I will plan for it not to last. I'll leave room for change. I'll learn to hop, so when the ground is pulled out from under me, I'm already used to unstable footing. I'll learn to put one foot on thin air, and then the other one, because that is where life is.

I learned that all I have is inside me and that nothing is under me. But I never really grasped that because it is so against my composition, so I just walk and put my feet down without any surety, and I hope and expect that one foot or maybe two will land on something.

Maybe that is faith.

I learned a textbook definition of faith in Sunday School. But I didn't *know* what faith was until I was out there and there was nobody with me and nothing under me.

Faith is believing in something you cannot see. Faith is that place where there is not even a cloud to stand on. There is thin air above you and only sky and thin air below you, and you've learned that God is there and you can't see him or even feel him sometimes, but all the solid grounding he has filled your cells and soul with over the years sort of holds you suspended in all that thin air.

We set the closing date, and my sister and I made plans to go home to 807 one last time.

Blog: "807"
Posted: March 1, 2010

My sister brought four air mattresses. We filled them and stacked them, two where my twin bed used to be and two where hers was in the room we shared all our growing-up years. We both wanted to spend one last night in the now-empty shell of a house on Deering before we closed the sale on Friday.

"Look, here's the ghost," I said.

"What ghost?" she said.

On our wooden bathroom door of the knotty pine room, the sap lines had run in the shape of what to me had always looked like a little man wearing a ghost-like robe with his long tongue hanging down. She had never noticed.

"Whatever happened to your white French dresser?" she asked.

"I think Mama sold it," I told her. She laughed and commented on how I had all my makeup in there and I'd told her not to touch any of it, ever.

"Did you?"

"Of course," she said.

I walked through the house and remembered. The casual dining room always had a chocolate cake in the cake dish in the built-in china cabinet. In the kitchen Mama was always frying something in a cast iron skillet on the front left burner of the stove. In the living room, our TV sat on the 1950s-style cedar chest that was now in my sister's attic waiting for my son to go get it. In the front bedroom, Mama and Dad both took their final breaths. In the middle bedroom were a stereo, a piano, a couch where I sat and talked on the phone every night during my high school years. And the back bedroom, my sister and I shared all our lives, from paper dolls and Monopoly to pep squad and sororities. I could look at the red blinking radio tower lights south of town from the window beside my bed. I could smell the honeysuckle on the back fence, and in the fall I could hear the cotton compress on Memorial Drive hissing and humming. Every night in the adjoining bathroom, I'd wash my face and put on Clearasil, roll my hair on jumbo brush rollers, and read my Bible in there so I wouldn't disturb my sleeping sister.

This place was where I became who and what I am. How do you leave this? How do you walk away from all these memories?

Friday morning, my sister put on a red sweater. "Oh my gosh," I said. "I have the same sweater in blue, and I'm wearing it today." We laughed and said, "Yes, we are definitely sisters."

One thing stood out: the house was too quiet. It was never quiet. Mama and Dad weren't here, and the silence rang in my ears.

Mama had told me once that when she grew up and left her childhood home, her father said to her mother, "The sunshine has gone out of this house." I felt the same way now.

135

I hung the old flag out front that Dad flew every patriotic holiday . . . the one I hung the day he died and then the day Mama died. The flag signaled all ends.

Judi and I went to the cemetery and told Mama and Dad a new family was going to be living in the house at 807. Then we signed on the line. And cried.

After the closing, I went back to the house to get my suitcase and my dog, and I took down the old worn metal numbers beside the front door—8 0 7—and carried them home with me and hung them up in my house where I could see them every day. I also dug up some of the monkey grass in the yard and put some dirt in a jar which I would later display in a crystal candy dish.

Multiple losses are hard. It's easy to cross a point to where you just cannot feel, process, or care, and you realize there are more loved things on the other side than this side.

I went home to Franklin and began cleaning out drawers in my own dear solid house. I knew I would be selling it, too, as soon as I found a new job, and I needed to thin out and throw away stuff we had accumulated. I began with the bedroom chest Charlie had used. In a bottom drawer was a long roll of architect drawings he had sketched himself for a contemporary house he'd built in a previous marriage. That dear solid house was one of the prides of his life— the fact he designed it and oversaw the building of it. I held the roll, opened it, and looked at the engineer print and the lines of rooms, and I wondered what I would ever do with it.

I took it out to the garbage can and carefully put it down in a corner space next to black bags, so it did not get wrinkled or soiled. In other words, I threw the plans away, but I took care in doing so.

When the sun went down that night and I went to sleep, the nightmare came. It involved Charlie, and he was angry, furious, and I woke up in a sweat. When light came, I went outside and retrieved the house plans and returned them to the bottom drawer. Cory told me a few days later that he'd had a nightmare about Charlie that same night and asked me what I had done to make him mad.

With March came the focus of finding work. I met with an employment company, the same one that found me the job I'd just lost, but it was a different agent, and she had her sweater on inside out, and I left knowing she was a scattered soul and it was a wasted effort. I contacted a former employer for a reference and ended up going to work for his company part-time.

A door had opened. I had a base income doing work that required skills that matched my experience, work I enjoyed, work I could do from home. But it was part-time, and it was up to me to fill the remainder of the work-week with something I'd always wanted to do.

All my life I'd worked for others with no control over my destiny. We moved, I lost a teaching job. I lost a job because a company downsized. I left a job to work for my husband, and he died, so that job was gone. I got another one and lost it because the company suffered an economic crisis and closed its doors. I was always at the mercy of others.

A networking lunch with another writer ended up with a decision to start a new business offering writing and editing services and a publishing solution. We established a business plan, secured domains, and developed a website. I'd be running my own company.

Still gnawing at me was the one big task I had yet to do: sell my house. I had to let some time go by and build a work history and prove income. Because I was self-employed, I needed to be able to show income for two years in order to secure a loan for a new mortgage.

I'd bought myself some time. Time to grow my business and do diligent work for my clients and prepare good financial records. Time to relax in my dear solid house and keep warm under Charlie's heated blanket and stay secure a little while longer.

A Second Letter to Charlie

Blog: "Passage: An Open Letter, Part 2"
Posted: March 23, 2010

My dear husband,

So much has happened. And you weren't here for it. At least not that I could see or touch. Oh yes, I think you really were here. I think you are the reason I have slept so peacefully and soundly at night. I think you have breathed your logic over me and helped me to carry on into the wind. I think you are the reason for my happiness instead of utter devastation after losing my job last month, when I faced no income. But you weren't here to physically hold my hand through it or to hold me and tell me it was going to be okay. You were always an anchor when I would be climbing the walls.

Two Christmases, and you weren't here. I bought myself gifts and drove seven hours to spend the holiday with Todd. The first year, Cory rode with me. This past Christmas, I drove alone. The first Christmas, we put your favorite Vols cap on the top of the tree. This past Christmas, we didn't.

Two Thanksgivings, and you weren't here. Remember those holiday Thursdays when our house was full of family? I know I fussed and grumbled about having to clean the house and cook all those desserts and side dishes, but how I loved it, down to the year I made that fancy pine cone spread out of cream cheese and whole pecans. The first Thanksgiving after you died, it was just Cory, Leah, and me. You never met Leah.

She came from North Carolina to be with Cory when you died and he was falling apart, and she came to your funeral and ordered the director to move out a TV and bring in a table so we could set out your pictures. You would have liked her. The second Thanksgiving, I spent alone, *yes, alone*, in Cleveland, in my mother's empty house one month after she died, getting it ready to sell.

Oh, and you weren't here for that either. My mama died. It was a grueling death, and you weren't here to hold me and tell me it was going to be okay. I did her eulogy, and you weren't here sitting on the front row and giving me the thumbs up for being strong enough to get through it, like you did for my dad.

The twins will be one year old in two weeks. You never got to know about them. The process of in vitro was started a week after you died. My two grandchildren were born last April, and I was ecstatic, and it was all stuffed inside because there was no one to tell, and you weren't here to laugh with me and hold me down on solid ground while I flitted and floated and danced about.

Two Valentines Days, and you weren't here to bring a card and roses home, like it was going to be a surprise, but I knew you would do it because you always did. A day for lovers, and I had no flowers.

And the job I lost . . . I went to work seven weeks after you died because when you died, so did your company and the business we ran together. Last month, half of us were let go. You weren't here to listen to my daily tales about my colleagues. You weren't here to provide footing when all that was gone.

Oh, and I sold your GENISYS domain name.

After a trip to Mississippi last month, I drove back home up the Natchez Trace and cried like I have for the past twenty months. Then I decided I didn't want to do it any more. I'm tired of crying. Just tired of it. Yes, I still love you, and I miss you more than anything in this whole wide world, and I will always want you back. But you are gone. So I stopped at the Tennessee River, upstream from where I had dumped your ashes, and told you I needed to move on.

Not long after you died, I ordered a book of poems, *March, before Spring*, by Stephanie Mendel, who had lost her husband, too, and I read them all. And cried, and understood. Every word, every feeling of the grief experience. Until I got to the last poem.

"Suppose I moved your photo . . ."

What?

"Suppose I were walking on a bridge that began to sway too much and I ran to the other side instead of heading back."

It rattled me.

But time works its way.

And I want you to know I have moved your picture.

Yours,
Kathy

Riffles, Runs, Pools, and Strainers

After the losses I'd had, I wasn't afraid of a little risky behavior. What did it matter? I could sit behind my computer monitor all day or lie in bed and die. I'd just been through death, and it was a common part of my life now. I didn't have the filters and boundaries I'd had all my life. I needed to do something wild and crazy.

Cory and Leah both kayaked in the fast rivers of North Carolina. Leah worked in outdoor recreation at the University of North Carolina in Asheville and led kayaking expeditions. They took me paddling on the Duck River. I borrowed next-door-neighbor Ken's red canoe, and Leah and I paddled together. We put in at River Rats, just off Highway 431 in Maury County, and we paddled nine miles, four hours, down a gentle leg of the river that flowed between lush tree-lined banks, tall bluffs, and rocky cliffs. We were on part of a thirty-seven-mile stretch that was designated a State Scenic River, beginning at Iron Bridge Road near Columbia and extending upstream to the Maury/Marshall County line. All sorts of shells lined the banks and filled the bottom of the river. We saw wildflowers, such as foamflower and bamboo grass, we saw caves in the limestone bluffs, and there were sycamores and rope swings all along the way. It was beautiful and peaceful—a splendid ride!—and I wanted more of the water. I was happy on the water.

I wanted something totally unlike me—something edgy, daring, and fun. I wanted a one-man boat. I bought a kayak. I got it the year after Charlie died, the month before Mama died.

I chose a recreational design, without a watertight skirt, because I didn't want to worry about rolling over. So if my boat turned over, I would just fall out. Cory and Leah helped me search online and in local sports stores. Then Cory found a kayak in Hickory, North Carolina—a yellow Heritage Featherlight with a wide, stable design that would track easily and sit on the water without making me feel like I was going to tip.

"I'll drive over there and get it, and Leah and I will bring it to you on your birthday."

I agreed to that. I trusted him with my purchase, without even seeing it first. I bought a paddle to match, and Cory gave me a PFD—personal flotation device—that I mostly referred to as a PDF, like the computer documents I created for work.

The three of us took our kayaks to the Narrows of the Harpeth on Labor Day weekend to test mine out. The Narrows was an easy jaunt west of Nashville to Kingston Springs. The water was flowing at 79 cfs, a quiet ride, but it was always moving. There were riffles and faster-moving places, and there were beachy areas, turtles sunning on logs, and some high rocky cliffs. It was my baptism into kayaking, and I had two experienced paddlers showing me the ropes. I got the hang of it and loved the challenge of moving straight down the river, looking for the V in the water and following the current. I loved sitting on the stream's surface. I loved the sound of the water dripping off the paddle. A great blue heron flew ahead of us, treetop to treetop, leading the way.

I learned about strainers. A strainer is a downed tree or a log pile—some huge clog in the river. The water's force is greater in a strainer—water could flow through, but the paddler could not. It would trap a paddler and hold him under. But rivers also hold riffles, where the water is fast at the surface with waves and splashes; runs, where the water moves fast but calm; and pools, where the water is deep, slow, and calm. Life for me was a riffle, swift and choppy at the surface, and I wanted to get to a pool and be at peace.

I was hooked on the water.

Eleven months after the Nashville area thousand-year flood of 2010, we took our boats out on the Harpeth River in Franklin for a short ride. We put in at the Rec Center, and we'd take out at Cotton Lane, which was in my neighborhood. The Rec Center put in was steep—stairs that went straight down—and I didn't like it one bit. The river water was high that day, though, so it was easier to get in the boat. Cory held my kayak while I stepped in. I had to turn circles and work to keep my boat stationary while he and Leah put in. We paddled, took pictures, watched birds, practiced skills, and fussed about all the garbage in the water. The Harpeth was trashy before the flood, but afterward, it was filled with junk—an old rusty car, plastic chairs, tires, plastic bottles and tin cans, and natural debris like fallen trees and somebody's cornfield that got washed away.

We moved downstream in the twisting, coffee-colored flow, by the bridge on Hillsboro Road, and then through the southern part of Fieldstone Farms, my neighborhood of two thousand homes. I'd been looking at houses to buy and would've liked one that backed up to the river. I could go out in my back yard and put the kayak in. But that dream ended after the Flood of 2010. Those houses were filled with river water, and I'd never trust living there.

We were nearing our take out, and I kept looking ahead for the bridge off Cotton Lane. We'd get out just before the bridge and carry the boats up the embankment. If we missed it, we'd have to . . . paddle backward.

Then I saw something ahead. A strainer? A big strainer.

"Strai-ner!" I liked shouting it out to show that I knew the word. "Look at the debris way ahead," I said. I kept trying to see an opening that we could paddle through. "Is it . . . blocking the river?"

I saw Cory's eyes look left, then right, and his eyebrows tightened.

"You stay here," he said. "Keep your boat way back here. Paddle in circles, paddle backwards. Don't get anywhere near that. We'll go check it out."

They paddled to the left bank, then across the river, which was moving faster up there and making a whooshing sound, over to the right bank, then back toward me.

"It's blocked. There's no way through," Cory said. Leah nodded. "What do we do now?"

"We'll have to take out here, climb this bank, walk around the blockage, and put in on the other side. We're almost to Cotton Lane, so it will be a short run."

I looked at the embankment. A dirt wall. Straight up. Maybe twenty feet. Or thirty.

"I don't think I can get my boat up that cliff."

"Leah and I will get all the kayaks up, then I'll come back down and help you."

"I'll be fine. You worry about the boats. I'll get up by myself."

They took me up on it. What had I gotten myself into?

We scrambled for the boulder-lined water's edge. I was last to get my kayak nosed in between rocks so I could get out. I stood and put one foot out on a slippery rock and tried to keep standing without sliding. I had one foot still in the boat, and the boat started moving downstream. I was doing the splits, and I tightened every muscle in my thighs to keep my legs from moving further apart and to hold my boat. Cory reached for me and grabbed my kayak.

I watched as they climbed, Cory with two boats, and Leah with hers. He got to the top, threw the boats up, and pulled her up. It was a difficult climb, even for the younger ones.

Then it was my turn. I could see the two disappearing into the woods with the boats.

"Y'all don't worry about me. I'll be fine," I yelled after them. They didn't seem to be worried.

I started scaling the dirt-mud cliff. I pushed a Chaco sandal into the earth and clawed into the dirt with my fingers. There was a clump of weeds, and I grabbed hold. The plant began coming out of the earth. I had to pull at one plant, then grab another. There were no saplings or sturdier plants to use in my climb. I got halfway up and looked back down at the stones below and the water moving fast. I looked up at the top of the hill, and there was a contemporary house nestled under trees not far from me. It had walls of windows. I imagined someone inside looking out at this poor, crazy woman struggling up the straight side of the cliff, fearful of her being dashed onto the boulders below, and wondering if they should call 9-1-1. I wished they would.

I began to fail myself, thinking I needed a rescue squad to come pull me out. I was unsure about going higher. I looked back down at the water moving fast over the jagged rocks. I knew I had to do it. There was no other way out. I took a deep breath, took on new strength, and pushed myself upward, grunting with each foothold. I grabbed onto any little green thing growing out of the mud wall, watching and groaning in fear of the earth releasing it.

Then Cory was there at the top.

"Come on, Mama!"

I sank back into weakness. "I can't do this!"

"Yes you can. You've got to."

I could feel my face hot and red, I dug my feet in, tightened my leg muscles, I pulled at the clumps of green, and got to where he could reach me. He held down a hand.

"Grab hold!"

I reached up, and he pulled me to the solid surface, and I clawed into the dried grasses on top to secure myself. I made it, and as I lay there on my stomach, arms outstretched, I wanted to cry from the emotion of it all.

Needless to say, it wasn't a peaceful run. We were spent, strained, hot, sore, and hurting, and we still had to put in and take out again.

I would realize later how much like grief this little outing was.

I was moving along gently down life's way, following the peaceful sounds of the river and tracking through the choppier places, gliding over riffles, runs, and pools, and suddenly, there was a strainer. The water could move on through it, and I couldn't. I was knocked out of the flow.

I was at the bottom of a ravine looking for a way out.

I couldn't get out of this without hard effort, without clawing the dirt walls and getting mud under my fingernails and grunting and groaning and yelling out in pain and agony and pulling myself up bit by bit—pulling and climbing and sliding back some—until the dirt was smeared all over me, and I clung to weeds with shallow roots and tugged some more and waited for those fragile stalks to give way and drop me down again because I didn't know if I could make it out. But I kept trying, I kept looking at the top, and I saw a hand reaching down for me.

A hand. Reaching down. For me.

The Last Big Thing

I waited a year and four months. Then I called the same realtor as before, got pre-approved for a loan for a new house, and made repairs and staged my Wimbledon house. In July, 2011, my realtor put a For Sale sign in my front yard. The house listed for twenty-five thousand less than it would have the year before. The housing market was still in a spin, and it was still a buyers' market.

The listing brought showings, but much of the feedback indicated that lookers didn't like my floor plan. I thought the floor plan was its biggest asset. It was good for empty nesters because they could live downstairs without ever going up and save the upstairs for company. It was also good for people with older children because there were two big bedrooms and a bath and a bonus room upstairs—a kids' second story. I didn't really care if nobody liked it, because if a buyer never came, it justified my staying there. And I wanted every excuse to stay there.

Then on a Saturday in October, I had two repeat showings. One, I just knew was right. The woman's husband had died exactly one year to the day after Charlie died. It was one of those tidy life packages I used to live for, and I just knew God had tied the bow around that perfectly wrapped box. But it was the other looker who offered a contract. The family had two dogs, liked my back yard, wanted my doggy door, and the floor plan worked for them.

It was going to happen. My house was going to sell. I had to find a new one.

My realtor scheduled appointments to show me houses in my price range. My friend Judy went with me on Sunday afternoons to look. She had been a realtor in Mississippi and knew what to look for and what questions to ask. We found a new subdivision of all-brick homes with three houses in progress on one street. Three other houses on the street were already occupied and another had sold, but was not yet inhabited. The housing market was just starting to come back and new construction, which had been stopped for three years, was gearing up. Two of the houses in progress on this street had porches—I wanted a porch!—but all the bedrooms were upstairs, and I did not want that. The third house being constructed had a small porch-entrance and all the bedrooms were down. It had a large bonus room up, which could be my office with space for a desk, credenza, and bookshelves, and there was also room for a sitting area with my futon couch which could double as a bed for extra company. The master bedroom was big with a beautiful trey ceiling, a huge closet, a commode room, tub and shower, and a vanity with double sinks. The house had a dining room, which I wanted so I could keep having company on holidays and so my writing group could come and sit around the table and critique stories. It also had a great room, a breakfast nook, a kitchen with granite and stainless steel appliances, two extra bedrooms, a second bathroom, and a big deck. It had everything I wanted—except a porch. And I could live without that.

The completion date for the house was the same date as the closing on my Wimbledon property. Another one of those tidy life packages, and I was certain God was taping the ends of the wrapping paper on that box. My realtor negotiated a contract for me.

The process was in motion. No stopping it now.

Before final approval of my loan, I had to write a letter to my bank and explain why I was buying a smaller house: "I am electing to downsize—to buy a new place that is smaller and easier to manage, both physically and financially, for the rest of my life. It is a wise and calculated decision to do this, as well as good stewardship of my time and resources, both now and in the future."

This was not just a move. It was a moving on. I was ready for it. I was not ready for it.

Grief is not something you get over. It's a mantle you wear—a figurative cloak that covers even the clothes you have on. It is the image you present to the world. Life happens all around you, and over time you realize a need to not snap that mantle around you anymore and give it life. You take it off, you fold that mantle, store it on a shelf in the closet, close the door, and hold only to the memory of it.

I was ready to do that. I was not ready to do that.

I had already sort of done that in a way. I had taken the giant step (after I said I never would!) of going out on a date with a man, an old friend who'd lost his spouse, too—out to dinner, then to a movie, to a Shakespeare play, a rodeo, a theater production, an outdoor symphony, and to the ocean.

I could feel Charlie nudging and encouraging me. He was ready. Three and a half years was long enough. He needed to move on, and I needed to move on.

Selling the house was the last big thing. I knew it would be an end—the end of a beautiful chapter of my life. No, I wasn't ready to let it go. Leaving, I'd be going alone.

That's what this journey was all about. Being one and feeling complete. Being me and feeling confident in my own choices and decisions. Being able to say "my" instead of "our."

Moving On

F all always made me think about mazes, like pathways between hay bales stacked in high walls, with dead-ends that made me turn back to find a new option, until I discovered the doorway out.

Franklin used to have Earl's Fruit Stand three blocks off the square on Franklin Road between Dotson's Restaurant and the Harpeth River. It was more than a stand, though, with rambling ramshackle indoor rooms full of harvested goods. Earl had fresh vegetables, fruits, peanuts, honey, jellies, flowers for spring planting, Christmas trees, and anything else he could sell. Come fall, he had pumpkins, a biggest-pumpkin contest, and a maze of hay walls for kids to work their way through. Squeals came from inside those walls, sometimes cries of panic, and laughter. I took my kids there when they were young and walked through with them. They were better at finding the way than I was.

Fall itself is a passage, when the world moves from sun, heat, and green to drifting leaves of red and yellow to brown settled in piles under bare trees. Fall passes into winter, when the work is done and it is time to go inside and rest.

Come fall, my house on Wimbledon Circle had a maze of brown moving boxes, taped, sealed, and labeled, running down the hallway and through all its rooms. From the time a contract was put on my house, I started boxing things up—little items from drawers, cabinets, and bookshelves, things I could do without for two months—because I knew what an overwhelming job packing would be for one person.

But boxes or not, come Thanksgiving of 2011, I was having company, inviting all the family, because it was the last Thanksgiving in the Wimbledon house. In the early years, my parents were there, and Charlie's mother, Louise, came the first year we were married, just seven months after her husband died, and every year after that for as long as she was able. David and Ruth always came, and Ruth always brought deviled eggs. Sometimes nieces and nephews came. My sons were there, then a daughter-in-law joined the family, then twin grandchildren.

This year was a far cry from that first Thanksgiving after Charlie died, when there were only three of us. Nine people came, and the big fat Butterball turkey slathered with apricot preserves and Jack Daniel's Old No. 7 Brand Tennessee Sour Mash Whiskey went in the oven at five in the morning. When it was time to cut the meat, Cory picked up the knife and went to work. David said the blessing, we filled our plates, then sat in a dining room with brown boxes stacked three high against its walls. Afterward, the boys threw a football in the back yard, and I sat on the patio in an Adirondack chair, looked up at my old pasture trees, bare of leaves, leaves on the ground, watched Jillie and Hardy, two now, run and play in them, and felt the wind on my face. This was a great house for having grandchildren in. I hated to leave it.

My closing date was nine days away. I had a lot to do in a short span of time. I had to finish boxing up the pictures on the walls, a hundred unmatched pieces of Tupperware, a hundred little cans of spices, down to the tiny box of toothpicks. I had to pack up every detail of my life for transport, even the heavy wood-slatted chair I was sitting in. One reason I put off moving was that I didn't think I could do it.

"Do y'all want to go see the new house?" I asked the kids.

"Yeah, sure, let's drive down there," Todd said. They all wanted to go.

"You won't get to go inside because it's a holiday, and the house is locked, but you can at least see where it is, see the outside, and look in the windows."

We squeezed into Todd's Suburban and drove down Highway 31 through rolling hills and pastureland with cows and horses to a new subdivision. The maples lining the main neighborhood street were blazing red, and the sky was a deep blue. And to my surprise, three men on the paint crew were putting the final coat on my walls on Thanksgiving Day. My family got to walk through my new house.

The next week I packed up the Lenox china, Solitaire pattern. Friends came and packed up the kitchen, the Christmas decorations, and all the books. I did the rest of the house myself.

I'd been cleaning out, throwing out, burning in the fire pit, selling, donating, and giving away items for three years, but the attic was still full, the garage was fuller, and two storage spaces held stuff from the childhood of my sons. Cory had graduated from college in North Carolina and lived there for eight years, but he still had a room full at my house—his Cargo bedroom furniture we bought when he was seven, a full closet, even a tux, a desk with art and sketching materials, his swimming trophies and medals, even the Easter basket I painted bunnies on when he was two. "You need to come home and clean out your room," I'd kept telling him. "Because if you don't do it, I'll have to." He made a few feeble attempts, but not even a dent. "Don't throw anything away," he told me. I ended up reducing that one big bedroom down to two boxes and then with his permission, gave the furniture to Todd for my grandson.

In order to get from the Wimbledon house to the new house, I'd had to apply for a loan, provide information and documentation of income, hire movers, inform utility companies, and change my address with every vendor. It was a full time job.

I couldn't slow down for the season. This Christmas would be the first year ever that I wouldn't decorate a tree. In my house there were no signs of Christmas. There were only brown boxes, some packed and stacked and forming mazes, some empty and flat on the floor, waiting to be filled.

It made me think back to Christmas of 1986. My father had had a heart attack two days after the Pearl Harbor anniversary—the attack that took him to war. This time, though, he was fighting a critical battle for life, air-lifted out of his Mississippi Delta town to Baptist Memorial in Memphis. He had quintuple bypass surgery six days before Christmas. My family spent most of that holiday season at the hospital. In the lobby there were hundreds of red poinsettias strategically stacked in the tall three-dimensional shape of a Christmas tree, a large circle of plants at the bottom, tapering, rising up to one red plant at the top, and all I saw was a reminder: Emmanuel, God with us. God with us during this frightening life change. How I needed that reminder at a time when my foundation was being shaken.

Now, the walls of my life had not only shifted, they were gone. Everybody older and above me was gone, and I was at the top of the pyramid. I'd made it from the bottom to the top, I was the matriarch of the family, and it was lonely up there.

The dog was all I had with me at the Wimbledon house, and the Wimbledon house was all Chaeli had ever known. I'd taken her to the new house with me, let her walk around on new sod in the front yard, up and down the sidewalks, all through the house in its progressing stages of completion, trying to give her some transition. For weeks in our Wimbledon house, she watched me turn flat sheets of cardboard into boxes and strip tape around them and pack them and strip more tape. She kept looking at me, fully aware that something big was going on. Our stuff disappeared and the stacks of boxes in the house grew, until we were nothing but boxes.

My house closing day was set for Friday, December 3, and moving day was Saturday, December 4.

Friday afternoon, I sat in a lawyer's office in Brentwood, low light, dark furniture, white papers with black print being pushed at me. It took five minutes to close on the Wimbledon house, and I didn't even see the buyers. I signed my name, and it was done. Then I had to work through a stack of papers for the new house, sign my name on each one, and as the signed stack grew higher, so did my excitement. It was a pretty house, brick in muted browns, brown plantation shutters, lots of windows, white trim, a floor plan fit to me. Not only was it brand new, but it was perfect. Sand-and-finish hardwood floors, shiny white molding, taupe-colored walls—perfect. Not one scratch, dimple, or nail pop.

I couldn't help but think about the contrast of moving into the brand new Wimbledon house sixteen years earlier, when the construction crew never finished it. My punch list from the initial walk-through wasn't addressed for the final walk-through, and the punch list from the final walk-through was a page and a half long, most items never checked off. On moving day, painters were inside the house trying to patch up walls, and the movers were pointing out bad places for them to fix and shaking their heads at the incompetence. The trim on the outside back of the house was four different colors. The painters had used whatever was left over from other houses on the street. The porch rail was never installed, and the lattice for the windows was never put up. After we moved in, I told the crew to just forget it—I liked it better without all the trimwork anyway. And if all that wasn't bad enough, they didn't even hook up the master bathtub, which drained dirty water under my house for three weeks till I discovered wet bricks at the foundation and called them on it and called City Codes, too.

Now, this new house. Perfect. Just perfect. I made a good decision buying this house.

Saturday morning at eight, the movers arrived. I put the dog in her crate in the living room, where she could watch all the action. She began to shake and progressed to a violent tremble. She didn't understand what was happening, what it would mean for her, what the day would bring.

This move was all about endings. Up until now, that was it. Endings. Boxing up, packing up, purging, throwing out, giving away things attached to that person who was no longer with me, keeping some, remembering, letting go. Crying, hurting, fussing at him for being a packrat and holding on to everything that I was having to throw away or pack up and move. Then turning the lights off and driving away from the Wimbledon house, closing a chapter of my life.

And driving to the new house.

As I began to unbox the pots and pans and build a hill of white packing paper on the kitchen floor, the dog walked over, stepped into the stack, rattled it, circled, and lay down. Then she looked up at me, and her brown eyes said, "Okay, I'm in this, too." I loved how she looked at change—shook and suffered through it, sized it up, and took it for what it was. After all, what choice did she have? I'd packed up all her beds, blankets, collars, food bowls, and fancy jackets and put her down on the hardwood of the new brown-brick and she had to get used to a whole new life.

The first night in my new house—MY new house—I fell exhausted into bed and pulled the covers up around me. I looked out the bedroom door into the little hallway and across the family room, and I could see the double doors in the breakfast nook that opened to the deck. I could hear the drone from the interstate a mile away, the hum of the heater coming on, and I turned my fan on for its white noise. The dog stood up on the bed, re-circled, then plopped down and pushed against me. My bedroom had a double window, uncovered now, because I didn't have time or energy to hang up a sheet or buy temporary blinds. Faint light came from a streetlamp a house down. I lay there and looked out across the street at two white lighted reindeer forms on the front lawn, one moving its head up and down, as though eating grass.

What better reminder than to see the lights of Christmas in yards around me passing on the message: "Emmanuel, God with us."

God with me during this life change.

This Christmas, everything was new, and it was a time for rebirth, time to start over, or to start recalculating time.

Now in the new house, I think about beginnings. New people, new stores, new everything. I needed new. I needed change.

Kathy Rhodes

Blog: "Destinations"
Posted: December 18, 2011

Three and a half years, I've been on a journey. It wasn't a trip I had planned, but it was a trip I had to take. And now I've done the final big thing—selling *our* house and buying *my* house. From *our* to *my*. That characterizes the journey.

So how fitting that when unpacking boxes in my new brown-brick house, I pulled out the old grief workbook and held it for a few minutes instead of putting it away on a shelf. I couldn't help but give in to the distraction, look inside it, turn the pages, chapter to chapter, and read the answers I had written down during sessions of grief recovery. In black-ink cursive I had formed words that instructed me on how to walk through grief:

I had to accept that my husband died and wouldn't be coming back.

I should hold on to and store my memories of him and our life together because in time, emotional remembering shifts to historical remembering, and that is sweet.

I needed to deal with and let go of all my emotions—anger, sadness, fear, guilt, regret, loneliness—and cry out the tears of anguish and agony.

I had to uncouple, to separate my own identity—it's not "we" anymore, it's "me." The journey is from "our" to "my."

I had to relearn life, realize I am living in a new normal, and reinvest in life.

Reinvest? I just bought a new house!

Then I realized . . . I've done it. I've completed these steps to recovery. The first three were never much of a problem for me. It was the last two. Emotionally, I didn't want to go from "we" to "me." I didn't want to give up my old life. I wasn't ready. I will never be ready. I just had to do it—make a good decision with my head, then walk behind that decision and let my emotions follow.

156

This is not to say that when I lay claim to this grief book and open it and see my handwriting all over the pages, my emotions don't plunge back to the depths, because they do go straight back to that time when my "bones were in agony," when I had "a tingling that rolled down from the backs of my arms, leaving me weak all over, and legs that didn't want to step forward." When my heart pounded and I had to get the grief out, and so even late at night I'd go outside and run and weep and let my warm tears mix with a cold falling rain.

There's no way around grief. There's no way it can't absorb you. You have to walk down that road, through that valley the Twenty-third Psalm calls "the shadow of death," through a trench with walls higher than your head, a trench that snakes through the earth, a trench with twists and turns and dead-ends, and if you are knocked into that trench, you learn to embrace what happened to you and shoulder into the pain. You cry until all the tears are gone, then you cry some more. You keep working at it, and one day you realize you have reached the doorway out. You are there in a well place.

In time, padding grows between the present state of mind and the past raw emotions early in the grief journey. There's some distance between you and your loss. The things you've had to do during that time to stay on the swift-moving merry-go-round of life (that doesn't slow down for you to get off and back on again) have kept you in the game. Mundane things like paying the electric bill every twelfth of the month, choosing new tires (two or four?), renewing the car tag every May, filing quarterly estimated income tax, and going to the grocery store every week and buying his brand of paper towels or laundry detergent or mayonnaise, or your favorite kind. The revolutions spin you, you try to keep some balance, and meantime, you are not only moving around in circles, you are moving forward. This is how you get to "my."

Dear Lord, I don't remember his favorite brand of mayonnaise.

A Maze and the Well Place

L ife prepares us for where it takes us.

When my little sister was two years old and the whole family would go somewhere in the car, Judi would turn around in the back seat and look out the back window, and when we'd turn the corner at Deering and Fifth, she'd start to cry. "I can't see my house," she'd say. She needed to see it to know it was there. Mama would tell her it was there waiting for her to come back in a little while.

Faith is believing in something you cannot see. Believing in a power that held you up in the past and that you have held fast to. Because you have experienced that power, you know it is there, in you, under the pain and cobwebs and dust and black holes of your life, and that is enough, for now.

In the early days after loss, I couldn't hold on to my faith. The hum and buzz of grief covered up any rational thought or any awareness that I was being held in the palm of God's hand. I felt alone.

I looked around me at friends and even strangers. There were only couples. Twos. It got to where I wouldn't go buy groceries on Sunday afternoons because there were only couples in the store. Never single people. The marrieds weren't working on Sunday, so part of their together time was spent shopping for food. My best friends were part of a couple relationship. They didn't know loss. They didn't know loneliness. They didn't even think it was in the cards for them.

It was like loss had been directed at only me. Healing can't come with that thought. It was only when I began looking outside me that I realized tragedy comes to others in different ways at different times. A little girl was killed at an intersection during the Christmas holidays. If the other car had gone out of control a week earlier, the child would have been in school and spared. Sometimes it seems as if all the cards are stacked to deal a tragedy to an unsuspecting soul, leaving loved ones shattered. When you think about it, in the case of a car accident, both drivers have to leave their beginning points at precisely the right second in order to meet head-on at a certain fixed point. The stars have to be aligned to make it happen. And it does happen every day. And then there are those OnStar moments, like that man who went to play golf had—the husband of the woman I met at the Franklin hospital who shared her miracle with me. Why do some people get tragedy and others get OnStar moments? Why do good people, people who go to church and read their Bibles and pray, get tragedy laid in their laps? Why did Charlie's artery tear? Why did the sky fall? I had to get beyond that.

The laws of the planets and the universe don't make exceptions for good people. One day for no reason a cell goes haywire and grows into a malignant tumor and changes a life. A car spins out of control and hits a tree or hits another car, whatever is in its path to stop it, and turns a life upside down. Good people get ill and injured as much as anyone else.

There were good things that happened to me after tragedy got dumped in my lap. It took me a while to realize that my faith knew God was taking care of me. Doors opened—two jobs, money to pay the bills, a buyer for my old house, an approved mortgage for a new house. I had to keep walking that grief road to arrive at a fixed point on it that let me see that even though God didn't intervene and stop the horrific process that killed Charlie, he was present with me and letting some good things happen.

I spent time on that grief road, and grief is messy and chaotic and mean. Grief is more like a maze of emotions than a road that runs straight from town to town or from the bottom of the valley to the top of a mountain. Just like in a maze, I moved forward a bit, ran into dead-ends, and then turned back and traveled over the same route until I found light at the end of the tunnel. "God hath not promised smooth roads and wide, Swift, easy travel, needing no guide . . . God hath promised strength for the day, Rest for the labor, light for the way . . . ." (Annie Johnson Flint)

I needed a softness in my heart. I wanted it, and I let my heart walk toward it.

Grief is a journey to a new configuration of life.

I can pray now. I can pray for others. I can pray for myself.

I can see my house now.

I have found that well place in my heart. The place that lets me take hold of what I have known was always there.

Life Changes Again

I t was ten o'clock and time for bed. Holding the phone to my ear and talking to my friend, Neil, I turned off the dual computer monitors on my office desk, then headed down the stairs. As I descended, I noticed there were long strips where tape seamed drywall pieces together at the ceiling line and midway down on the hall wall. The tape was lifting. I'd been in my new house four months, three weeks, and one day. It wasn't ever like that before.

"Something's wrong," I told Neil. "The drywall tape is visible, you can see it all the way down the hall, it's puffed out. I just looked up and saw it. It's something I would've noticed before."

April the twenty-sixth was an unusually hot and humid day. Rain and storms came. A tornado touched down in Franklin in the city park where kids were playing baseball. They were safely removed from the field ten minutes before the funnel cloud appeared. High winds flipped cars at the park, blew down the scoreboard, and caused injuries to two people in a Jeep that overturned.

"I can mash it. It's puffy. And crinkled at the edges." I touched it with one finger, tapped it lightly, and it was soft, and it pressed in. "I think there's . . . water . . . behind it. There's a leak somewhere." I tried to swallow and couldn't. A cold, hot, hollow, sinking, rising sensation came over me. "I've gotta go check this out."

I put the phone down and ran back up the nine stairs and climbed into the attic, which had an access from the office closet. I knew I should check the air conditioner condensation pan to see if it was overflowing. That happened once in my old house. The pan overflowed with condensation water, which ran across a board, down on the ceiling, and dripped to the furniture and floor of the bedroom below. But all was dry here in my overflow pan. I didn't know what was going on.

The next morning at eight sharp, I called the builder's office, and in twenty-four minutes from across town, Phil, the warranty manager, pulled his truck to a stop in front of my house. He moved quickly to diagnose that a condensation pipe in the air handler in the attic was leaking. He shut the air off in that part of the house and called the HVAC company that had installed the unit.

Two technicians went up to the attic with Phil. I climbed up there, too. Dad had taught me by example that this was what you did when something broke and somebody had to fix it. You stood right there with them and watched. And made sure they did it right.

"We gotta replace the whole thing," one of the technicians said, and laughed.

"What?" I said.

"I told you guys, no joking around here," Phil said, holding up his hands to stop their play. This was serious.

"Yeah, I'm the owner, and I'm up here listening to this."

They had the little pipe replaced and the unit fixed in fifteen minutes. Then the warranty team removed wet insulation from the attic and assessed the damage caused by the water.

"There's a little white pipe that caused the leak," Phil said. "It was manufactured out-of-round at the factory. There's a tiny hole that water leaked through. There's nothing anybody could've done about it. Just one of those things."

Part failure.

Because the unit was installed during cold weather and I bought the house in December, the air conditioning was never tested, even by the private inspector I had hired.

I knew that even if the air conditioner had been checked in December, it wasn't warm or humid enough to show a condensation leakage problem. I also knew that I'd been using the air for two months, so it had apparently been leaking in small amounts during all that time—onto attic floor boards, down a framing board behind the drywall in the hall, onto the subfloor. April the twenty-sixth came hot and humid enough to incite a massive amount of condensation. I understood all this with my head, but not with my heart or any other part of my being.

Phil stood next to me and looked down at his feet. Then he held his hands, palms out, toward the hall. "To do this right, I've got to take down the drywall in the hall and replace it, then re-paint it."

It felt like my throat fell on top of my stomach. I tried to muster some bravery. "Then. Go ahead." I choked on the words. I wanted it done right. But it was my *new* house. Now there was part failure, and all the newness was gone. "I've got to be able to get through the hallway, though. I've got to work upstairs while you're fixing this."

The sixteen-foot hallway and stairs led to my "bonus room" office, and my income depended on my being in the office all day.

"No problem," he said.

He came back the next morning and started tearing out drywall. I sat at my computer and tried to concentrate on my work. I listened to hammers and bangs and nail pulls and creaks and rips as the wall came down. I wiped the tears streaming down my face and smeared them on my keyboard as I typed. I tried not to look. I didn't want to know what was behind the wall, didn't want to see the skeleton, didn't want my house bared to its foundation. I just wanted to see the whole of it. But I had to walk down that hall many times during the day. I had to look at the core—the studs, the raw wood, bent nails, splinters, places in the wood that got hammered too hard.

Out of seventeen hundred houses the builder had constructed during his career, I was one of two with major issues. It was a great record for the builder, but what did it say about me? As one of the boys from the HVAC company told me, "If it weren't for bad luck, you wouldn't have any luck at all."

"I'm going to call Will over here to check the floor," Phil said. "He can take up a few boards and make sure it isn't wet under there."

Dear God, oh God, please God, not my beautiful sand-and-finish hardwood floor. God, can't you give me a break somewhere and stop this madness and let me have just a little bit of normalcy?

All I wanted was peace. I moved to a brand new house because I didn't want to have to paint the walls, pull up carpets and put new ones down, or deal with the worn wood flooring of an older house. I paid more than I really intended in order to get NEW. I wanted—needed desperately—to move in, get my stuff in place, and live a quiet life. My house was my office, too. I wanted to move in and do my writing and editing job. I wanted to move in and move forward with my own personal writing.

I wasn't going to get what I wanted.

Will came and pulled up a few boards in the hallway. Wet.

Then I asked the question, the one question that changed the course of everything. "If it's wet on this side of the wall in the hall, what about the other side of the wall in the kitchen?"

The warranty team pulled out the stove, and Will pulled up a board. Wet.

"This is bigger than we thought," Phil said. "It needs to be an insurance claim. We'll file it with the HVAC company's insurance."

I hadn't even unpacked all the boxes from my move four months ago, especially in the garage, because I had to fit it in with a heavy workload, and now I was looking at days or weeks of repair work interruptions, plus I had to take down pictures I recently hung, move furniture that was in the way, and pack up the contents of the kitchen drawers and cabinets.

Maybe it was a sin to love this new house so much. To keep looking around with pride and claiming perfection, beginning to worry I wouldn't find anything to put on a one-year warranty list for my builder to fix. Everybody had a punch list—bulleted items to be addressed during that new-home warranty period. I hadn't found anything yet. I promise, the house was perfect.

The dark, heavy thoughts were already starting to come at me. Not only could I not keep my husband alive and do that right, I couldn't even buy a house right. What was wrong with me?

Everything—*everything!*—I touched went wrong.

"Here's the pipe that caused all this," Phil said. He placed the eleven-inch white pipe in my hand. Round smooth plastic piping, with curves and white purity, like a new bride in a silky white gown. "See that?" He pointed to a connection where two pieces fit together. There was a hole in that bridal gown, an imperfection, a gap like a sliver of moon at the end-fitting where the pipe was out of round. There was an opening smaller than the crescent tip of the nail on my little finger. You could see clear sealer that wasn't spread adequately enough to cover the little hole.

Part failure. It seemed that everything in my life had had part failure and either died or broke. Why me? Why not one of the other seventeen hundred houses? I didn't need to go there, I shouldn't have gone there, but I couldn't help it. After all the losses I'd suffered over the past three and a half years, I could go nowhere else. *Why did bad stuff keep happening to me?* It seemed I was doomed to live with part failure. And I was doomed to live with the end results after part failure.

Sometimes life takes you by the throat with both hands, cracks the cartilage, and throws you breathless to the ground. It seemed life couldn't let anything good happen and last.

Some of the floor boards were already beginning to cup. All the hardwood in the hallway would need to be pulled up, plus the wood around the corner in a short passageway to the breakfast nook, plus half the kitchen. The granite counter tops would come off, the cabinets would be removed after their contents were packed up, and the stove and refrigerator had to be moved out.

Workers from the particular trades dealing with each component would be scheduled in sequence to handle each step of the process. But first, a restoration company would need to come in and make sure the wood was dry.

Because this repair now involved an insurance claim, the warranty team was stepping out, and I was responsible for hiring contractors to fix my house and then paying them individually with the insurance money. I begged the team to stay, but the scope of work was too large for them. It was too large for me, too.

I spoke with the insurance representative for a plan to proceed, and I interviewed three restoration companies, hired one, and they came and set up a dehumidifier in my breakfast nook and two large turbo fans in the kitchen. The fan motors roared like a rushing river for four days. I couldn't even hear the phone ring. The constant sound pushed me further to the brink of insanity.

I unraveled. There was no way I could find, hire, schedule, direct, and manage multiple contractors and still work my usual ten-hour days.

My friend Judy called to check on me. I had shared my disaster with her. When she learned the warranty team had backed out and dropped the entire repair project in my lap, she took on my anger. Judy's former career was in real estate in another town, another state. She'd moved to Franklin from Greenwood, Mississippi, after her husband died. Jim died five months before Charlie. Judy and I were put in touch with each other by my high school and college best friend, Gerri, who worked for Viking Range, where Jim was a VP. Judy had first looked at this house with me on a Sunday afternoon search. She and I had bonded on our grief journeys. We'd attended a grief group together at Brentwood Baptist Church, and we talked about things with each other that we didn't share with anyone else. We had the kind of relationship that we could say what needed to be said. She could get tough with me when the situation called for it.

"No," she said, "that's not right. You call that builder. You call him right now. You hang up from this call and call him. Don't wait one minute. I mean it. You call him right now. You tell him he's got to get back on this. Will you promise me you'll do it?"

"Yeah," I said, thinking I wouldn't. I didn't want to call him. I didn't know what to say. I was too defeated to make that call.

"I mean it. I'm going to hang up now and you call him, and I'm going to call you back and see if you did."

I hung up and cried.

I was experiencing complicated grief, starting all over again dealing with loss, the loss of my new house now.

I could feel it, a little composite ball, rock hard at the bottom of my gut, rolling around through pity, hurt, anger—rolling, picking up emotions, getting bigger—bitterness, despair, failure—bigger and bigger—frustration, isolation, worthlessness—growing thicker and rounder, this mix with a texture like black mud, grit-sand, and gravel. It was pushing against the sides of my humanity. I was doing my best to hold it in. As it grew, I started to take on a fear of everything. I was afraid to buy anything. I was afraid to drive anywhere. I was afraid to ride on the back of my friend Neil's motorcycle anymore, knowing full well that if anything bad could happen, it would, and I would be ruined, maimed, or dead. A cold resolve started to settle in. Nothing good would ever happen to me and nothing would ever happen at all unless I became hardened and steeled and fought tooth and nail for it.

I called. That gritty ball filled me up, and in a mix of tears, heaves, and breathlessness, I sobbed it all out. "I have a job. I can't do your job of fulfilling warranty repairs. It's not my fault the pipe failed. I don't know the contractors to hire, I don't understand the construction process, I don't know what to do to make this house right again. I need you to do your job and get your team back in here to fix my house like it was when I bought it four months ago."

He immediately and compassionately agreed. He understood. He got the warranty team back in.

For forty-one days, my house was taken down to its feet, back to its original state in some places, and then built back.

My stove was in the garage. My refrigerator was hooked up in the living room so I could use it. I put a coffee pot in my bathroom. Coffee and filters stood next to the Noxzema and hair spray. Paper bowls, plastic spoons, and a box of Cheerios were there beside a hair brush and a flat iron.

When it came time to sand and finish the floors, the hardwood men put plastic sheeting up to divide the living area from the kitchen and breakfast room. To get to my office or the kitchen or to wash a load of clothes, I had to go out the front door, open the garage door with the remote, walk by the stove and car, and in the back door to the utility room. There were times when I couldn't get to my office at all, like when the floor was drying. I was told beforehand when these times would be, and I worked late nights, early mornings, and weekends to accommodate. It was a difficult situation, but the warranty team workers made it as smooth as it could have been and went over and above what they had to do to get the house right again. And then after everything was sanded, stained, wall boards up, walls painted, trim painted, everything clean and neat and back in its place, they hired an air doctor to come and check for any possible mold or other organisms growing.

Finally, in June, two weeks before my scheduled vacation, this long process of undoing and redoing was over, and I could put things back in order, get settled, and have some peace. And rest in the knowledge that I had a new home and things were working right.

Then I realized that this process was what I dealt with every day in my own work—peeling something back and restoring it even better. I did this with stories, as a writer and editor. My own stories. The stories of others. I could deal with this analogy and understand it.

I also realized this was what had happened to me in my losses. Life had boiled what was in my crucible down to the salt of me.

My life had been peeled back to just my bones, a bare skeleton. It was up to me to add meat to those bones. I had to build anew. I had to be able to exist in this new normal, this new life I was somehow building all around me without even knowing I was building a new life.

Hammer. Nails. Build it. Paint it. Live in it.

I smiled as I realized that when the storm came, when the rains fell—the disaster caused by that little white pipe—my self emerged, just like it broke out of an immature larval shell, and it separated from the wisps of what I had believed was Charlie's lingering spirit here in this realm. Before this disaster, I felt Charlie with me, and I would talk to him, ask him questions, and tell him of my progress, thinking he'd be proud of how I was making it. I'd even talked to him about buying this new house. Maybe I had been hanging on to the past just a little bit. With this leak, though, I became my own force and handled it alone.

That was the final step of uncoupling.

A Whole New Life

May 28, 2013

It's climbing to eighty-eight today, and I am out in it. I brush a line of deck stain across a step and watch it soak in to the weatherworn wood. The phone I've taken outside with me rings, and I reach for it, getting the brown color on my old Franklin jazz festival tee shirt.

"I hope you're not outside in this heat," Cory says.

"Yep, I'm right out in the middle of it. I'm sealing my deck."

"Take breaks, go pee, and check the color of it. If it's dark, drink more water."

You never know what you will hear from a son who's an EMT. He tries to take care of me, and I am trying to take care of my house.

The deck wood cupped last summer because it was raw and new to the elements, and the elements were severe—weeks with no rain and temperatures over one hundred and relentless sun.

The Southern yellow pine this deck was made from came from Shuqualak, Mississippi, pronounced Sugar Lock. There's a stamp on each piece of lumber that tells me its origin. This is the place of my ancestry. My great-great-great-grandfather got an original land patent beside the Noxubee River near Shuqualak and moved there in 1833 after the Dancing Rabbit Creek Treaty was signed, allowing white settlement in Mississippi.

In 1850 my great-great-grandfather bought land a county south, in Kemper, and my great-grandfather, grandfather, and father grew up on that land. I visited there as a child and played in woods with trees thick as hairs on a dog's back, my dad always said. Now, I own some of that land. I have a pine plantation there. I cut timber a few years ago. This deck could be made out of wood from my family land. I feel like I've come home.

Next to the step I'm painting is a light purple iris I dug up from my grandmother's yard on that family land. I like to pull meaningful things in tight around me. That's what I've tried to do with my husband. I feel guilty if I don't give his life a presence. And it is okay to do some of that. But it is the attachment to him that causes suffering, the holding on that extends the grief period. So I've had to figure out what to hold on to and how to present it in honor and memory of him and how to move on.

And so I have bought this house and built this yard with my own two hands. And this year, its second spring, what I'd hoped for is happening. The landscaping has come back strong. Following the rule of perennials—the first year they sleep, the second year they creep, the third year they leap—the plants are all creeping, and they are creeping well. Last year when I planted them, they were just tiny things in big beds covered with mulch. Their little roots were embedded in that awful clay dirt my house sits on. When it's wet, it's slippery wet and packed tightly. When it's dry, it's pottery. How can tender plants grow in hard pottery?

I kept working on that soil. Last fall I aerated and overseeded. I put down lime. I put down seasonal fertilizers and weed killers. Every time I planted something, I'd add topsoil with peat and conditioners. I worked diligently on this plot of land made of compromised and unhealthy clay, not dirt.

Now you'd never know my yard was clay. This spring the grass came back lush and high, dark green and thick, so thick it has to be mowed every three days, and all the bare spots are covered. Flowers are popping out all over. The blackberries, muscadines, strawberries, and blueberries are bearing fruit. This season I have a hummingbird feeder, and hummingbirds are visiting. I put up a bluebird house, and I have a family with young. I bought a new

171

birdhouse at the Franklin Main Street Festival—yellow and cobalt blue with a rusty Celtic cross on it—and I erected it in the northwest quadrant of the medicine wheel garden above the red yarrow. The mint has come back strong and filled its wedge of the wheel.

In one year, the yard is full and growing and healthy.

It's beautiful.

The medicine wheel, a circular formation outlined with stones and with stepping stones in the shape of a cross in the middle of it, was said to be a sacred space by early Native Americans—a place for meditation, a centering device. To me, it is a reminder—it makes me think of where I came from, who I am, and where I'm going. It reminds me to keep in tune with self and soul. A medicine wheel is said to bring wholeness and happiness.

I think back to the night Charlie died, when my sister told me, "You've got to build a whole new life."

One month from today it will be five years since Charlie died.

Now I am not "that woman who lost her husband." I'm more than that. I'm more than what happened to me. I am a builder of new things.

I have built a whole new life.

Next to the step I'm painting, the wind chimes ring, a heavenly sound, bold, loud, and strong.

Spiritually, I am enough to approach God. On the deepest level, I was never a couple to God. I stood alone at his throne.

I am building back spiritually, too.

Why do bad things happen to good people? I don't know, but I think the answer is that there is not an answer. Sometimes things just happen. Sometimes processes are set in motion by the realities of the world we live in: genes, environmental hazards we're exposed to, asbestos in our old schools, the "mosquito man" spraying DDT from the back of his truck we all chased when we were kids. Cigarettes. Winston Rand and his Winstons.

At first, after the surgeon at the hospital in Franklin told me that Charlie would not survive without divine intervention, and I prayed and begged, but God did not intervene, then that set up some contention between God and me. In my fragile state, I was afraid to pray for a time after that. If I prayed, then surely the opposite would happen. But I came around. I polished that nugget I'd been holding and carrying with me for five years, all jagged and grainy. I smoothed off the spikes that pierced me and saw that bad things happen to *all* people. Good things happen to all people. Good life happened all around me, and I got caught up in it.

My good thing now is that I have found a resting place far from my sorrow. Now I stand at the threshold of the future. I will go forward and upward.

I remember the dragonflies from last summer.

Those magnificent aerialists above my deck, they could hover, dive, fly backward, downward, forward, and upward. They started out as water creatures, submerged in the dark, then gradually, in time, found their way to the skies. Their metamorphosis describes my journey these last five years. I have survived the darkest time of my life and found my way onward and upward.

I get up from my deck staining to go inside, and as I reach for the door, I notice for the first time that on the mat above the WELCOME, there's a dragonfly shape, all sun-faded adobe, yellow, and white.

June 27, 2013

I am on vacation with my sister and her husband and his two sisters, and there are seven of us in all traveling together in Canada's Maritimes. The trip's last two days mark the fifth anniversary of Charlie's dissection and death. I've written about my journey through grief and healing and decided to title it *Remember the Dragonflies*.

Dragonflies have become special to me because of their symbolism. Once a dragonfly climbs out of the water, gets wings, and takes to the skies, he cannot go back into the water. He's in a new realm. He cannot return to the old realm in his new form. He can't get in the water with wings.

Like Charlie. He's in a new realm, too.

And me. I'm in a new place, a well place.

I've been telling Charlie I need to hear from him again. I need him to come back to me in some way on that five-year mark of his passing from one realm to another. I need a sign. I need some physical connection to him. Or I want it. It's the way I'm made. It's the "me" who likes the answers to life's questions wrapped up in a tidy package with a pretty bow around it. It was up to him to figure out how to come to me.

At the beginning of vacation week, on the road to see the *Anne of Green Gables* house, we stopped by the two-thousand-square-foot showroom of Gaudreau Fine Woodworking Artisans, halfway between Charlottetown and Cavendish on Prince Edward Island. The shop also features the works of twenty Maritime potters. In a far corner on display were a few pieces with a dragonfly etched in them. I picked out a square plate in dark earthy tones of sage, olive, gray, and black. I could set this plate on a display stand, and it would be a reminder of Charlie, of my grief journey of uncoupling and building a whole new life, of my book.

It is five years to the day after Charlie's aortic dissection and we visit Peggy's Cove, a small fishing community on the shore of St. Margaret's Bay in Nova Scotia. The landscape of Peggy's Cove was carved by the migration of glaciers. Four hundred million years ago, movement of the Earth's crust allowed molten material to bubble up from the interior, forming big rocks. The melting and movement of the glacial ice left scouring marks in the bedrock, still visible today. Scars, like the death of my husband left on me. Sitting atop the rock is a lighthouse.

As I walk away from the lighthouse, across the parking lot of the Sou'Wester Restaurant and Gift Shop, I see an injured dragonfly on the concrete. It is brown-speckled with clear wings, still alive, still trying to flap its wings. Its lower abdomen has either been run over or stepped on and is stuck to the surface, and the dragonfly will eventually die. I can't just leave it there to be run over again. I pick it up, put it on the flat palm of my hand, and it walks to the tips of my fingers like it is going to take off and fly away into the heavens, but it doesn't. I take it to the grass beside the parking lot and give it a resting place on the cool green next to a big rock.

I cry, and the tears soak my face. Because it is June the twenty seventh, and here is a dragonfly for me. Some say dragonflies are the souls of the dead. Some say the deceased send us dragonflies to give us reassurance. Is this Charlie coming to me, or just a coincidence? Is it a tidy miracle box wrapped up as a gift for me? Some would say I am crazy to think so. But I believe it was meant to be.

Later, in Lunenburg I shop at Window to the Sea, where I find a necklace with a bronze coin stamped with a dragonfly. I buy it as a reminder of Charlie, my grief journey, my book.

June 28, 2013

Five years today.

Today we drive up to Maitland to go tidal bore rafting on the Shubenacadie River with a company named River Runners. A guide will take us out on a motorized Zodiac boat past eagle nests, Acadian dykelands, and geological formations to ride waves up to ten feet high as the tide rushes in. The Bay of Fundy is home to the highest tides in the world, creating the Shubenacadie's tidal bore. The bore is the first wave in, the point where out-flowing river water and incoming tide water meet, creating a powerful wave that forges upstream and causes the river to change its flow. This image depicts how life moves along in its own direction and death comes crashing into it and a violent surge takes life backwards for a time.

The River Runners office has a porch across the front and hanging on the wall are three silver, metal-like dragonflies, each about four feet long.

The staff sends us over to Bing's Eatery for a quick lunch before our rafting excursion. Bing's is a gathering place that combines visual art, music, and conversation with good food and drink. The walls of the dining room are covered in original paintings, all for sale. I keep noticing a big, colorful, abstract piece on the front wall, and as I finish my gourmet pizza, I realize it is a blue dragonfly among a chorus of other colors. My sister goes over and takes a picture of it, then says, "You should go look at the name of the painting." She laughs. I walk over and read the title/author tag. The piece is named "Genesis." Like Charlie's beloved business name: GENISYS.

Genesis. An origin, creation, beginning. The dragonfly symbolizes new beginnings. It represents self-realization and maturity and a letting go of the past.

At River Runners we dress in orange full-flotation survival suits, walk out across the mud flats to the water, find spots to sit on the edge of the Zodiac, and hold on to ropes positioned along the sides of the boat. Then we head up river ahead of the advancing tide to wait for the bore to form. When it comes thundering in, we'll meet it head on and then surf and jump the succession of surges, as the calm river turns into churning rapids. But first our guide takes us to a large sandbar and instructs us to get out of the boat and walk around on the brick-red sand.

"In two hours," he says, "the sandbar will be under thirty feet of water."

I lean over and write my name in the sand with my finger and then draw a dragonfly—one long swipe, two loops for wings on each side.

In a matter of minutes, KATHY and the dragonfly are under water and wiped away from the surface.

I hang on for the ride of my life. The waves slam against me. The water soaks me, even filling my ear as it slaps the side of my head. I move with the rocking of the vessel. The rope blisters my hands as I hold on with all my might, and I make it without washing out of the boat.

This summer I'll be looking for the dragonflies in my yard. And when they come, I will reach up to them, both hands to the skies, and touch their magic and laugh and dance with them.

You, too, watch for them.

Remember the dragonflies.

About the Author

Kathy Rhodes writes creative nonfiction and is author/ editor of three books. Her essay, "An Open Letter," appeared in *The Best Creative Nonfiction, Vol. 3* and was singled out for a review in *The New Yorker*. Her essay, "The Wedding Hankie," was included in *Chocolate for a Woman's Soul II*. Rhodes is founder and senior writer/editor of TurnStyle Writing, Editing & Publishing Solutions. She earned a BA in English from Delta State University and pursued graduate studies at the University of Memphis. She teaches creative nonfiction workshops locally and regionally and speaks to grief groups. Rhodes lives in Williamson County, Tennessee, where she kayaks on slow, twisting rivers and gardens in her back yard.

CPSIA information can be obtained at www.ICGtesting.com
Printed in the USA
LVOW12s1831271013

358655LV00003B/3/P